Grammar
Plus 1

Roy Kingsbury

 LONGMAN

Contents

1 Subject pronouns

I am Liz Baker

Singular	Plural
I	we (= you + I)
you	you (= you + you)
he	they (= he + she + it
she	or he + he,
it	etc.)

1 We always write *I* as a capital.

2 *you* is both singular and plural in English.

3 We use *he* for men and boys, *she* for women and girls, *it* for things and animals, and *they* for men and women, boys and girls, things and animals.

1 *Say* I, you *or* we. *Then write them.*

1
...You... are a student.

2
.... are Mr and Mrs Baker.

3
.... am John.

4
.... am Mog.

5
.... am Scamp. And .... ?

6
.... are John and Jane.

2 *Find the opposites in A and B.*

A   young   beautiful   short   strong   clean

B   ugly   old   tall   dirty   weak

Write your pairs here.

..... young – old ....

....

3 *Say* he, she, it *or* they. *Then write them.*

1
...She... is young.

2
.... is tall.

3
.... are clean.

4
.... is dirty.

5
.... is old.

6
.... are short.

7
.... is beautiful.

8
.... is strong.

Indefinite article *a / an*

Indefinite article *a / an*

We use **a** / ə / before a consonant sound:	**a** banana, **a** bird, **a** cat, **a** dog, **a** fish, **a** mouse, **a** parrot, **a** pineapple, **a** teacher
We use **an** / ən / before a vowel sound (a, e, i, o, u):	**an** ant, **an** apple, **an** arm, **an** elephant, **an** egg, **an** engineer, **an** eye, **an** ice cream, **an** octopus, **an** orange, **an** owl, **an** umbrella

The indefinite article **a / an** means 'one' and is only used in the singular and with a singular verb: It **is a** bird. / She **is a** teacher. / He **is an** engineer.

4 *Say he, she or it and a or an. Then write them.*

1
.It. is .a. mouse.

2
She is an artist.

3
...... is ...... octopus.

4
...... is ...... bird.

5
...... is ...... actor.

6
...... is ...... teacher.

7
.... is .... engineer.

8
...... is ...... policeman.

9
...... is ...... ant.

5 *Say and write the sentences.*

1 A penguin is a bird.

2 ....

3 ....

4 ....

5 A mouse is an animal.

6 ....

7 ....

8 ....

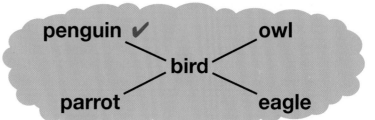

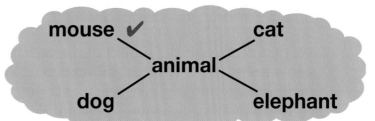

6 *Circle the odd word out.*

1 he   they   it   (ant)   we

2 owl   parrot   cat   eagle   penguin

3 apple   egg   dog   ice cream   orange

4 short   strong   old   young   she   dirty

2 The verb *be* (present simple)

She's a witch

This is Liz's birthday party.
It is a fancy dress party.

DAD: Who are you, John?

JOHN: I'm a king, Dad.

DAD: Who are Mike and Sarah?

JOHN: They're Batman and Robin.

DAD: And who is Liz?

JOHN: She's a witch.

DAD: Who are you, Jane?

JANE: I'm an actress. I'm famous.

LIZ: No you aren't. You're just a baby!

JANE: I'm not! I am an actress.

DAD: All right, children.
　　 Look at Scamp.

Affirmative		Negative	
Full form	**Short form**	**Full form**	**Short form**
I am	I'm	I am not	I'm not
you are	you're	you are not	you aren't
he is	he's	he is not	he isn't
she is	she's	she is not	she isn't
it is	it's	it is not	it isn't
we are	we're	we are not	we aren't
you are	you're	you are not	you aren't
they are	they're	they are not	they aren't

1 We never leave out the subject of the verb in English. We never say ~~is an actress~~ or
~~are a baby~~. We say **She is an actress** or **You are a baby.**

2 In affirmative and negative statements the subject goes in front of the verb and is
either a noun or a pronoun. We cannot use a name *and* a pronoun, so we can't say
~~Jane she is an actress.~~

3 We form the negative by adding *not* after *am, is, are* — *am not, is not, are not*. The
short forms of negatives are usually made with *n't*, **except** with *I*, which is *I'm not*.

1 *Fill in the blanks with* is, is not, are *or* are not.

1 John .....is..... a king. He is not. Batman.

2 Mike and Sarah .... Ghostbusters. They .... Batman and Robin.

3 Liz .... a witch. She .... an actress.

4 Jane .... a witch. She .... an actress.

5 Scamp .... Captain Strong. He .... Spiderman.

2 *Say these sentences with* **am, is** *or* **are.** *Then write them.*

1 You ...are... young.

2 She .... old.

3 He .... not an engineer.

4 We .... weak.

5 It .... a bird.

6 I .... not very strong.

7 They .... brother and sister.

8 She .... a student.

3 *Say these sentences with short forms. Then write them.*

1 (It is) ....It's.... a pineapple.

   (It is not) ..It isn't.. an apple.

2 (I am) .... a student.

   (I am not) .... a teacher.

3 (He is) .... tall.

   (He is not) .... short.

4 (It is) .... a bird.

   (It is not) .... an animal.

5 (They are) .... clever.

   (They are not) .... silly.

6 (She is) .... an actress.

   (She is not) .... an engineer.

Interrogative	Short answers	
	Affirmative	**Negative**
am I ...?	Yes, I am.	No, I'm not.
are you ...?	Yes, you are.	No, you aren't.
is he ...?	Yes, he is.	No, he isn't.
is she ...?	Yes, she is.	No, she isn't.
is it ...?	Yes, it is.	No, it isn't.
are we ...?	Yes, we are.	No, we aren't.
are you ...?	Yes, you are.	No, you aren't.
are they ...?	Yes, they are.	No, they aren't.

We use short answers when the answer to a question is **Yes** or **No**. We leave out the rest of the sentence: **Is he an actor? Yes, he is. / No, he isn't.** We usually use short forms in negative short answers.

4 *Ask and answer these questions about the party.*
   Then write the answers.

1 Is John Batman?   No, he isn't.

2 Is he a king?   ....

3 Are Mike and Sarah Batman and Robin?   ....

4 Are they Ghostbusters?   ....

5 Is Liz an actress?   ....

6 Is Jane an actress?   ....

Question words *Who? What? How old?*

Who is he?

He's Captain Strong.

What is he? Is he a spaceman?

No, he isn't.

How old is he?

How old are you, Captain Strong? Are you 100?

No, I'm not 100 – but I am *very* old!

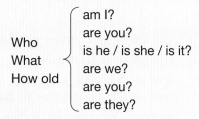

Who
What
How old
{
am I?
are you?
is he / is she / is it?
are we?
are you?
are they?
}

1 **Who?** is for people, but not for things. **How old?** is for people, animals or things.
2 In questions with questions words we use the interrogative form of the verb — **Who is she?** NOT ~~Who she is?~~, **How old are you?** NOT ~~How old you are?~~

5 *Make questions, then write them.*

1 she   is   who   ?

   Who is she?
   ....

2 are   they   what   ?

   ....

3 how   old   you   are   ?

   ....

4 he   an   actor   is   ?

   ....

5 is   what   it   ?

   ....

6 is   she   how   old   ?

   ....

7 dirty   are   they   ?

   ....

8 it   is   a   bird   ?

   ....

7   (seven)

6 *Join the words and make sentences. Then write them. Use full forms.*

1 <u>You are a student.</u>
   <u>You are clever.</u>

2 ....

   ....

3 ....

   ....

4 ....

   ....

5 ....

   ....

6 ....

   ....

7 *Match the questions and answers. Then write in the questions.*

Is it an animal?   What is it? ✔   Are they young?

Who is she?   How old are you?

1 <u>What is it?</u> ....   ·   It's a penguin.

2 ....   No, they aren't. They're old.

3 ....   She's a witch.

4 ....   I'm 10.

5 ....   Yes, it is.

3 Adjectives

A Quiz

1

a It's a grey mouse. ☑
b It's a white mouse. ❑

2

a It's a Greek stamp. ☑
b It's an American stamp. ❑

3

a She's a young lady. ❑
b She's an old lady. ☑

4

a It's a motorbike. ❑
b It's a mountain bike. ☑

5

a They are red pineapples. ☑
b They are red apples. ❑

I'm a clever cat!

Is Mog clever? **You** *do the quiz.*

A parrot is a bird. It's clever.	= A parrot is **a clever bird**.
He is a boy. He is good.	= He is **a good boy**.
It's an apple. It's green.	= It's **a green apple**.
It's ice cream. It's pink.	= It's **pink ice cream**.
She's a woman. She's old.	= She's **an old woman**.
They are girls. They're young.	= They're **young girls**.

1 The form of an adjective does not change in English: **old** is for men, women, things and animals, singular and plural: **an old man, an old woman, an old house, old bikes.**
2 Adjectives do not have an article in front of them when they are not followed by a noun: **He is <u>a</u> clever <u>man</u>** but **He is clever.** And we cannot say ~~**He is a clever.**~~

1 *Join the sentences. Say and write them.*

1 It's a cat. It's black.   It's a black cat.

2 She's a girl. She's clever.   ....

3 He's an actor. He's good.   ....

4 It's milk. It's fresh.   ....

5 They're dogs. They're big.   ....

2 *Make sentences. Say and write them.*

	tall	French ✔	policeman
2	red ✔	American	schoolgirl
3	big	English	car
4	young	Indian	stamp ✔
5	strong	Greek	elephant

1 It's a red French stamp.

2 ....

3 ....

4 ....

5 ....

3 **About you**

Describe yourself and a friend in the same way.

I ....

And .... , my friend, ...

4 Plural nouns

A poem

> And strawberries, radishes and tomatoes are red, too!

Giraffes are tall,
Mice are small,
Frogs are green,
And cats are clean.

Ice creams are cold,
Mountains are old,
Cherries are red,
And

Regular noun plurals

	Singular		Plural		Singular		Plural
1 Add **s**	cat	>	cat**s**	3 Change **fe** to **ves**			
	frog	>	frog**s**		knife	>	kni**ves**
	giraffe	>	giraffe**s**		wife	>	wi**ves**
	parent	>	parent**s**	4 Add **s** after -ay, -ey, -iy, -oy, -uy			
2 Add **es**	peach	>	peach**es**		day	>	day**s**
	radish	>	radish**es**		boy	>	boy**s**
	bus	>	bus**es**	5 But **y** after a consonant is **ies**:			
	box	>	box**es**		cherry	>	cherr**ies**
	tomato	>	tomato**es**		baby	>	bab**ies**
BUT photo > photo**s**,					lady	>	lad**ies**
radio > radio**s**, piano > piano**s**					fly	>	fl**ies**

With nouns which end in **s, sh, ch, x** and **ge, se, ze**, the plural is pronounced 'iz': bu<u>s</u>es, radi<u>sh</u>es, pea<u>ch</u>es, bo<u>x</u>es, bri<u>dg</u>es, ca<u>s</u>es, bree<u>z</u>es.

1 *Cover the poem and write in the missing words here.*

Giraffes...... are tall,

.... are small,

.... are green,

And .... are clean.

.... are cold,

.... are old,

.... are red

And .... are red, too.

2 *Say and write the plurals.*

1 A frog. Two ...*frogs*...   5 A beach. Two ....   9 An elephant. Two ....

2 A lemon. Three ....   6 A leaf. Three ....   10 A baby. Four ....

3 A box. Two ....   7 A glass. Six ....   11 A strawberry. Ten ....

4 A day. Four ....   8 A party. Two ....   12 A photo. Six ....

Irregular noun plurals

Singular		Plural	Singular		Plural
man	>	men	child	>	children
woman	>	women	foot	>	feet
policeman	>	policemen	tooth	>	teeth
policewoman	>	policewomen	mouse	>	mice
person	>	people	sheep	>	sheep

3 *Look at the pictures. Say and write the plurals.*

1

...*three feet*...

2

....

3

....

4

....

5

....

6

....

4 *This is a picture of a Korg. Label him.*

...*three eyes*...

....

....

....

5 Indefinite article *a / an*, definite article *the* and 'zero' article

It's a meal!

It's a very dirty T-shirt. Look. A white spot here. What is it?

And a big spot here ...

The white spot? It's milk.

The big spot? It's olive oil.

And two red spots here ...

Yes, the red spots are tomato ketchup.

And look! An orange spot. What is it? Butter?

No, it isn't butter. The orange spot is jam.

It isn't a T-shirt, Liz. It's a meal!

Indefinite article *a / an*	Definite article *the*	'Zero' article
Look, it's **a** spot.	**The** spot is on Liz's T-shirt.	It's milk.
Look, it's **a** red spot.	**The** red spot is tomato ketchup.	It's tomato ketchup.
Look, it's **an** orange spot.	**The** orange spot is jam.	It's jam.

1   **a / an:** We use the indefinite article **a / an** when we are talking about things in general and not about one particular person, animal or thing. **It's a cat** = one of many cats (not a particular one), or a cat and not a bird or dog. The indefinite article does not have a plural, so when we talk about many people, animals or things in general, we do not use an article (we use in fact the 'zero' article): **Frogs are green.**

2   **the:** We use the definite article **the** with singular and plural nouns when talking about a particular person, animal or thing: **The big spot is olive oil.**

3   **'zero':** With words like **milk, butter, olive oil, jam** or **coke**, we do not use **a / an** even if we think it is singular. We say **It's milk,** NOT ~~It's a milk~~.

1 *Look at the text and fill in the blanks with* **a, an, the** *or* **—**.

1 Look there's ...*a*... white spot here. What is it? — .... white spot? It's .... milk.

2 What are .... red spots? — .... red spots? They're .... ketchup.

3 Is .... orange spot butter? — No, it isn't .... butter. It's .... jam.

2 *Say and write the sentences.*

1

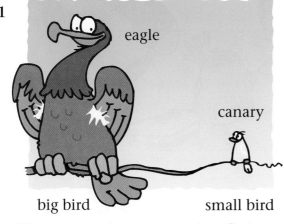

eagle

canary

big bird   small bird

The big bird is an eagle. The

small bird is a canary.

2

elephant

mouse

small animal   big animal

....

....

3

teacher

artist

the a an

short man   tall man

....

....

4

Mog
Scamp

cat   dog

....

....

3 *Circle the correct form.*

1 It is (an / the) cat.

2 I am (a / —) Liz Baker.

3 She is (an / —) artist.

4 (The / An) red spot is (— / a) tomato ketchup.

5 (— / An) eagles are (— / a) birds.

6 Who is he? – He is (the / —) John.

7 Is he (a / —) spaceman?

8 (A / —) frogs are green.

6 Imperatives

Do this! Do that!

DAD: Be careful, Jane. The rocks are slippery!
And don't lie in the sun, Liz.

MUM: Listen, children. It's lunchtime.
Wash your hands, please.
Don't go in the sea now, John.

DAD: Liz, don't throw sand at Scamp!
And don't run!
And listen, Scamp!
Sit there and finish your food!
Then lie down and sleep.

'Do this!'
'Do that!'
'Don't do this!'
'Don't do that!'
Parents!

Affirmative imperative	Negative imperative	
	Full form	Short form
Look!	Do not look!	Don't look!
Run!	Do not run!	Don't run!
Do this!	Do not do this!	Don't do this!
Do that!	Do not do that!	Don't do that!
Be careful! Be quiet!	Do not be silly!	Don't be silly!

1 The affirmative imperative in English is the same as the base form of the verb and is the same in the singular and plural: **Look!**
We add **Do not** or **Don't** to make it negative: **Don't throw sand.**

2 We often add 'please' before or after an imperative to make it polite:
**Please come here. / Come here please. /
Please don't do that.**

1 *Say these sentences. Then match them with the pictures.*

| Tidy your room. | Don't talk! ✔ | Don't watch TV! | Open your book. |
| Don't run! | Don't lie in the sun! | Please wash your hands. | Be quiet! |

1 ....
Don't talk!
....

2 ....
....

3 ....
....

4 ....
....

5 ....
....

6 ....
....

7 ....
....

8 ....
....

2 *Fill in the blanks with one of these phrases.*

| Don't play ... | Eat ... | Please wash ... | Please clean ... | Don't eat ... ✔ |

1 ....Don't eat.... the cherries. They're bad.

2 .... the glasses. They're dirty.

3 .... with knives. They're dangerous.

4 .... the strawberries. They're lovely.

5 .... your teeth. They're yellow!

3 *Read this shopping note.*

> Please go to the supermarket and buy 6 peaches, 3 lemons, potatoes and strawberries.

Now write a note for a friend to buy these things.

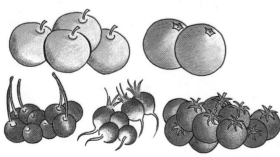

....

....

....

....

....

....

7 this, that, these, those

What's this in English?

A Spanish friend, Maria, is staying with the Bakers.

MARIA: What's this in English?
JANE: It's a wasp. Don't move!
MARIA: Why?
JANE: Wasps are dangerous.
MARIA: And what are these?
JOHN: These are bees. They're OK, but be careful.
MARIA: What are those in English?
LIZ: They're flies.
MARIA: And what's that in English?
LIZ: This? It's a cockroach.
MARIA: Ugh! It's horrible!

Affirmative

this is
that is / that's
these are
those are

Negative

Full form	Short form
this is not	this isn't
that is not	that isn't
these are not	these aren't
those are not	those aren't

1 We use **this** and **these** to refer to things, people and animals that are near us.

2 We us **that** and **those** to refer to things, people and animals that are some distance away from us.

3 Note (opposite) that in short answers we usually use **it / they** instead of **this / that / these / those**.

---

1 *Write sentences with* this is, that is, these are *or* those are.

1
This is a wasp.

2
That is a bee.

3
....

4
....

5
....

6
....

2 *Write sentences with* this isn't, that isn't, these aren't *or* those aren't.

1   (bee)   This isn't a bee. .... It's a wasp.

2   (mouse)   .... It's a frog.

3   (wasps)   .... They're bees.

4   (flies)   .... They're ants.

Interrogative	Short answers	
	Affirmative	**Negative**
is this ...?	Yes, it is.	No, it isn't.
is that ...?	Yes, it is.	No, it isn't.
are these ...?	Yes, they are.	No, they aren't.
are those ...?	Yes, they are.	No, they aren't.

Is that a French stamp?

No, it isn't. It's an English stamp.

3 *Ask and answer.*

1   Is this a wasp?   – No, it isn't. It's a fly. ....

2   Is that a cockroach?   – Yes, ...

3   Are those spiders?   – No, ...

4   Are these strawberries?   – Yes, ...

Interrogative with *What*	Answers
What is this / that? / What's this / that?	It is / It's a fly.
What are these / those?	They are / They're flies.

4 *Ask and answer these questions. Then write them.*

1   (this)   What's this? .... – It's a lemon.

2 (that)   .... – It's an egg.

3   (these)   .... – They're apples.

4 (those)   .... – They're tomatoes.

8 there is, there are

Captain Strong and the Korgs

This is the Korg Spacedrome. Where are the Korgs? Read this and number them.

Where's King Korg?

Look out! He's behind you!

1 There's a Korg under the spaceship.

2 Is there one on the rocks? – Yes, there is.

3 There isn't one near the children but there are two at the door.

4 There's one next to the spaceship.

5 There are three near the control centre.

6 There's one between the spaceship and the door.

Affirmative		Negative	
Full form	**Short form**	**Full form**	**Short form**
there is	there's	there is not	there isn't
there are	—	there are not	there aren't

1 *Say these sentences with* there's, there are, there isn't *or* there aren't.
Then write them.

1 There's a Korg under the spaceship.   5 .... a Korg near the children.

2 .... one in the spaceship.   6 .... two Korgs at the door.

3 .... two Korgs on the rocks.   7 .... one Korg next to the spaceship.

4 .... only one on the rocks.   8 .... three Korgs near the control centre.

2 *Correct these sentences about the Korgs.*

1 There are three Korgs under the spaceship.
   Wrong. There's one Korg under the spaceship.

2 There is one Korg near the control centre.

3 There are four Korgs at the door.

4 There are three between the spaceship and the door.

5 There are five next to the spaceship.

Interrogative	Short answers	
	Affirmative	**Negative**
is there ...?	Yes, there is.	No, there isn't.
are there ...?	Yes, there are.	No, there aren't.

3 *Ask and answer these questions about the Korgs with short answers.*
Then write them.

1 Is there a Korg under the spaceship? – Yes, there is.

2 .... four Korgs near the control centre? – ....

3 .... a Korg near the children? – ....

4 .... two Korgs at the door? – ....

5 .... a Korg next to the spaceship? – ....

Prepositions of place

Where are the flies?

There's a fly …

 in the soup

 on the apple

 **under** the grapes

 **near** the cherries

 next to the orange

 behind the lemon

 **between** the two spiders

4

> This is our village. There is a post office in Green Street. It's next to a restaurant. There are two restaurants in the village. There's a supermarket, too. The supermarket is in Long Street. It's near the garage.

Where are these? Say and write the sentences.

1 (library) There's a library in Green Street. It's next to a bank.

2 (garage) ....

3 (bank) ....

4 (school) ....

5 (station) ....

6 (park) ....

5 *How many of these are there in the picture – mice, knives, children, sheep, men, women? Where are they?*

1 There are two mice in the picture. There's one in a tree, and there's
   one under the table.

2 ....

3 ....

4 ....

5 ....

6 ....

6 About you

Answer these questions with full sentences.

1 What's the name of your street? My street ....

....

2 Is there a shop or a restaurant in the street? ....

....

3 Is there a bank or a post office near your house? ....

....

4 How many schools are there in your village / town? ....

....

Countables and uncountables; *some* and *any*

There aren't any mice!

JOHN: It's great here, Dad! Look. There are some white rhinos over there.

DAD: Yes, they're from Africa. There are only 11,000 in the world.

LIZ: Dad, I'm thirsty. Is there any lemonade in that bag?

DAD: No, there isn't, but there's some water.

JANE: Are there any ostriches here, Dad?

DAD: Yes, there are some over there.

LIZ: I'm hungry. Is there any chocolate in that bag?

DAD: No, there isn't.

LIZ: This zoo isn't very good. There aren't any mice or rats or snakes or insects or spiders!

DAD: Oh, Liz!

Countable nouns	Uncountable nouns
a hamburger, 3 hamburgers	meat, butter
a tomato, 2 tomatoes; a lettuce, 3 lettuces	milk, oil
a loaf, 6 loaves; a dollar, 10 dollars	bread, money
a bottle, 2 bottles	lemonade, water

1 **Countable nouns** are things, people and animals that we can count and they have a plural: **a hamburger, two hamburgers**.

2 **Uncountable nouns** are things like **water, milk, butter** that we cannot count. They do not have a plural and do not use **a / an**.

1 *Put these words in the correct columns A or B.*

milk ✔   a glass ✔   an ostrich   an egg   coke   butter   an orange

a potato   ice   toothpaste   olive oil   a sandwich

A Countable		B Uncountable	
a glass	....	*milk*	....
....	....	....	....
....	....	....	....

Affirmative	Negative	Interrogative
there is **some** cheese	there isn't **any** cheese	Is there **any** cheese?
there are **some** lions	there aren't **any** lions	Are there **any** lions?

1 **some** means 'a little' or 'a few' and we use it in affirmative sentences: <u>**some lions**</u> = a few lions; <u>**some cheese**</u> = a little cheese.

2 We use **any** in questions and in negative sentences instead of the word **some**: **Are there <u>any</u> lions? / Is there <u>any</u> cheese?**

2 *Ask and answer questions about the zoo visit. Then write them.*

1 any white rhinos / in / zoo?

Are there any white rhinos in the zoo? – Yes, there are.

2 any lemonade / in / bag?

.... – No, there isn't.

3 any ostriches / in / zoo?

.... – Yes, there are.

4 any chocolate / in / bag?

.... – No, there isn't.

3 *Look at the picture and ask and answer questions. Then write them.*

1 cheese / on / table? ...... Is there any cheese on the table? ....
No, there isn't, but there's some cheese in the fridge. ....

2 potatoes / in basket? Are there any potatoes in the basket? ....
Yes, there are. ....

3 bread / in / fridge? ....
....

4 tomatoes / in / fridge? ....
....

5 cherries / in / fridge? ....
....
....

6 grapes / near / chair? ....
....

10 Possessive adjectives *my*, *your*, *his*, etc.

Our new friends

JANE: Mum, this is my new friend. His name's Jason.

MUM: Hello, Jason.

JOHN: Mum, this is my new friend. Her name's Mary.

MUM: Hello, Mary.

LIZ: And this is my new friend, Mum. My snake …

MUM: Your snake?

LIZ: Yes, its name is Hiss.

MUM: Oh, Liz.

JANE: These are our animals, Jason. Their names are Scamp and Mog.

Animals?! We're family!

Pronouns	Possessive adjectives
I	my
you	your
he	his
she	her
it	its
we	our
you	your
they	their

These pairs of words sound the same when you say them, but look!

Possessive adjective	Pronoun + verb *be*
your	you're (= you are)
its	it's (= it is)
their	they're (= they are)

1 *Say the sentences with the correct possessive adjective. Then write them.*

1 I am John. ...My.. name is John.

2 We are Mr and Mrs Baker. .... names are Tom and Sue.

3 He is Jason. .... name is Jason.

4 You are the 'animals'. .... names are Scamp and Mog.

5 She is Mary. .... name is Mary.

6 They are my friends. .... names are Jason and Mary.

7 You are my friend. .... name is Mary.

8 It is a snake. .... name is Hiss.

2 *Say these sentences and circle the correct form.*

1 Its / (It's) my new book.

2 Their / They're white rhinos.

3 Your / You're tired.

4 Is that your / you're dog?

   What's its / it's name?

5 Their / They're our friends.

   Their / They're names are John and Mary.

6 This is my frog. Its / It's name is Greeneyes.

7 Is that your / you're dog?

8 These are their / they're bags — not those.

3 *Fill in the blanks with* **my, your, his, her, our** *or* **their.**

1 Where's the book for Liz? – ...Her.... book is behind the chair.

2 These apples aren't for Jason. .... apples are in the basket.

3 Where's .... camera? – Your camera is on the table.

4 Their names are Tom and Sue. .... surname is Baker.

5 The cherries under the oranges are for Mary and me. They are .... cherries.

6 Is this .... chocolate? – Yes, it's your chocolate.

7 His favourite colour is green and her favourite colour is green.

   .... favourite colour is green.

8 Where's my mouse? – I don't know. Where *is* .... mouse?

11 Possessive pronouns *mine*, *yours*, *his*, etc.

Where's mine?

DAD: Come on, children.
The food's ready.

JANE: Is there any for Jason?

DAD: Of course, Jane. Here's his
– and yours.

JOHN: Is there any for Mary?

DAD: Of course. This is hers.

LIZ: Where's mine, Dad?
And is there any for John?

DAD: Of course. Yours is all here.

MUM: And whose chicken pieces
are those, Tom?

DAD: They're ours.

MUM: Oh, thanks!

Possessive adjectives	Possessive pronouns	Possessive adjectives	Possessive pronouns
my	mine	our	ours
your	yours	your	yours
his	his		
her	hers	their	theirs
its	its		

1 Possessive pronouns are *not* followed by nouns: **It's mine**, not ~~It's mine book.~~

2 Possessive pronouns have only one form and are both singular and plural: **It is mine. / They are mine.**

---

1 *Say these sentences from the text and fill in the missing words.*

1 Is there any food for Mary? — Of course. This is ....*hers*.... .

2 Where's ...., Dad? — .... is here, Liz.

3 Whose chicken pieces are those? — They're ....

2 *Fill in the blanks in these sentences with the correct possessive pronoun.*

1 This is my food. This is ...*mine*... .

2 They are my sausages. They're ....

3 This is your hamburger. It's ....

4 These are your hamburgers. They're ....

5 This chicken piece is for John. It's ....

6 These chips are for John. They're ....

7 This lemonade is for Liz. It's ....

8 These sausages are for Liz. They're ....

9 This is our food. It's ....

10 They are our chicken pieces. They're ....

11 This is their food. It's ....

12 These chicken pieces are for Mum and Dad. They're ....

> Whose are these cherries?
>
> They're mine.

| **Whose** is this bicycle? | It's | { | **mine / yours / his.** |
| **Whose** are these books? | They're | { | **hers / ours / theirs.** |

This isn't my food. Where's **mine**? – **Yours** is in the kitchen.
These aren't her sausages. Where are **hers**? – **Hers** are on this plate.

3 *Look at the pictures and make sentences. Then write them.*

1 Whose shoes are under the table?
  My shoes are under the table.
  Hers are under the chair.

2 ....
  ....
  ....

3 ....
  ....
  ....

4 ....
  ....
  ....

5 ....
  ....
  ....

my shoes   her shoes

his house   my house

our milk   their milk

her sweets   your sweets

your coat   my coat

12 Possessive 's and s' and of

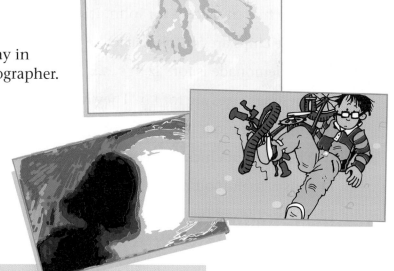

It's Mum's head

JOHN: These are the photos of our holiday in Greece – but I'm not a good photographer.
MARY: You're right! What's this?
JOHN: This? Oh, it's Jane's feet.
MARY: And what's that?
JOHN: That? It's Mum's head.
MARY: They aren't very good photos.
JOHN: No, they aren't. But this is.
MARY: Who is it? Is it your Dad?
JANE: Yes, it's a photo of Dad's accident!

Possessives

Singular – 's

It's John**'s** camera.
It's the cat**'s** bed.
These are the teacher**'s** books.
These are Mum**'s** dresses.

Plural – s'

This is the girl**s'** room.
This is the rhino**s'** food.
These are the boy**s'** books.
These are the animal**s'** food bowls.
This is the children**'s** classroom.

We use **of** (not **'s** or **s'**) with these:
This is **a picture of Mog**.

These are **photos of our dogs**.

1 We use the possessive **'s** and **s'** with people and animals to show possession or ownership. We use **of** with things.

2 Note the possessive **'s** with singular and plural irregular nouns: **This is the man's room. These are the men's rooms.**

3 We use **of** after words like **a picture, a photo, a painting**.
   It's a photo of Jane. = We can see Jane in the photo.
   It's Jane's photo. = The photo belongs to Jane.

1 *Make sentences from the conversation with these words. Then write them.*

1 these / photos / holiday / Greece
   <u>These are the photos of our holiday in Greece.</u>

2 it / Jane / feet ....

3 it / Mum / head ....

4 it / photo / Dad / accident ....

2 *Join the people and the objects and make sentences. Then write them.*

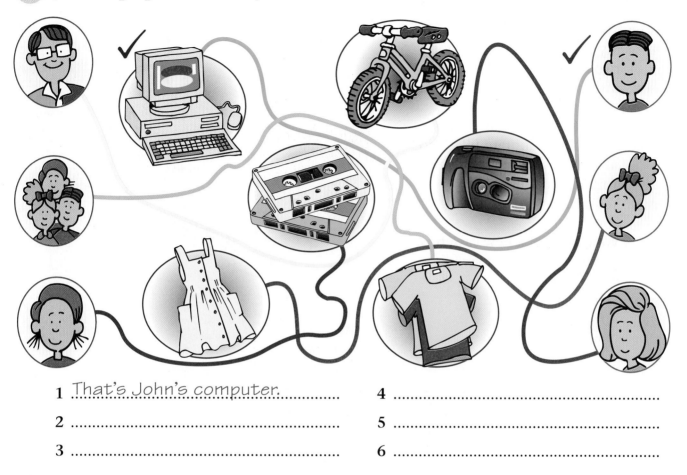

1 *That's John's computer.* ....

2 ....

3 ....

4 ....

5 ....

6 ....

3 *Look at the pictures and complete the sentences. Use these words.*

| elephant | fly ✔ | head ✔ | ear | cat | ears | lion | teeth |

1

That is *a fly's head* ....

2

These are ....

3

This is ....

4

Those are ....

13 has got, have got

I've got a mountain bike

JASON: My dad's got a new car.

LIZ: My mum and dad have got two cars!

JASON: My brother's got a motorbike.

LIZ: He hasn't got a motorbike. He's got a mountain bike!

JASON: I've got a mountain bike, too. And my sister's got a computer.

LIZ: You haven't got a sister!

JASON: Yes, I have – and she *has* got a computer.

LIZ: Well, I've got a new cassette player – and you haven't got one of these!

JASON: What is it?

LIZ: A frog!

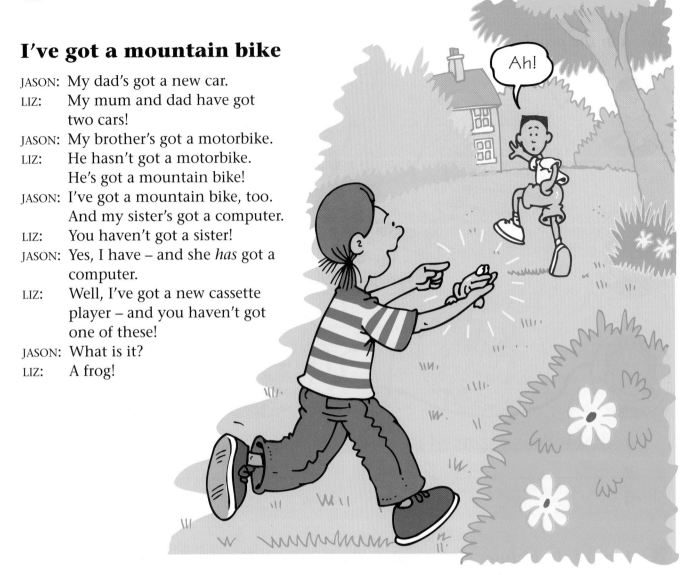

Affirmative		Negative	
Full form	**Short form**	**Full form**	**Short form**
I have got	I've got	I have not got	I haven't got
you have got	you've got	you have not got	you haven't got
he has got	he's got	he has not got	he hasn't got
she has got	she's got	she has not got	she hasn't got
it has got	it's got	it has not got	it hasn't got
we have got	we've got	we have not got	we haven't got
you have got	you've got	you have not got	you haven't got
they have got	they've got	they have not got	they haven't got

1 The verb **have got** only changes in the third person singular: **he/she/it has got.**

2 The short form of **has ('s)** is the same as the short form of **is ('s)**: <u>**She's** got a frog</u> = She has got a frog. <u>**She's a girl.**</u> = She is a girl.

3 We form the negative by putting **not** between **has/have** and **got**: **he has got > he has not got.**

1 Correct these sentences.

1 Jason's parents have got an old car.   <u>Wrong. Jason's parents haven't got an old car. They've got a new car.</u>

2 Jason has got two sisters.   ....

3 Liz has got a new computer.   ....

4 Liz's parents have got three cars.   ....

Interrogative	Short answers	
	Affirmative	**Negative**
have I got ...?	Yes, I have.	No, I haven't.
have you got ...?	Yes, you have.	No, you haven't.
has he got ...?	Yes, he has.	No, he hasn't.
has she got ...?	Yes, she has.	No, she hasn't.
has it got ...?	Yes, it has.	No, it hasn't.
have we got ...?	Yes, we have.	No, we haven't.
have you got ...?	Yes, you have.	No, you haven't.
have they got ...?	Yes, they have.	No, they haven't.

When we give short **Yes / No** answers to questions with **has/have got**, we leave out the word **got**:
Has he got a sister?
Yes, he has. / No, he hasn't.

2 Ask and answer questions. Then write them.

1 Jason / a brother?   <u>Has Jason got a brother? – Yes, he has.</u>

2 his brother / motorbike?   ....

3 Jason's father / a new car?   ....

4 Liz's parents / two cars?   ....

5 Liz / a new cassette player?   ....

6 Jason / a frog?   ....

3 Ask and answer these questions. Then write the short answers.

1 Has Jason got a sister?   <u>Yes, he has.</u>

2 Has his sister got a cassette player?   ....

3 Have his parents got a new car?   ....

4 Have Liz's parents got three cars?   ....

5 Has Jason got a mountain bike?   ....

What
- have you got?
- has he got?
- has she got?
- has it got?

4 *Ask and answer questions about the pictures on page 34. Then write them.*

1 John / a camera

What has John got in picture A? – He's got a camera.

Has he got a camera in picture B? – No, he hasn't.

2 Mary / a radio

....

....

3 John and Mary / sunglasses

....

....

4 the cat / black ears

....

....

5 John / a watch

....

....

5 *Ask and answer questions. Then write them.*

	lemonade	sweets	milk	apples	cherries
Jane	✗	✔	✗	✔	✗
Jason	✔	✗	✗	✔	✔

✔ = has got

✗ = has not got

1 Jane / lemonade? Has Jane got any lemonade? – No, she hasn't.

2 Jane / sweets? ....

3 they / milk? ....

4 Jason / apples? ....

5 Jane / cherries? ....

6 About you

Answer these questions with full sentences.

1 Have you and your parents got
a house or an apartment? We ....

2 How many rooms has it got? It ....

Has it got a balcony or garden? and it's ....

3 Have you got a cat or a dog? I ....

Have you got a bicycle? and/but ....

4 Have your friends got bicycles? ....

14 How many? How much? – not many, not much

A Silly Quiz

In pairs, ask each other the questions in this quiz and read out the a, b, c choices. Then tick the correct (or best) answers.

1 How many legs has a spider got?

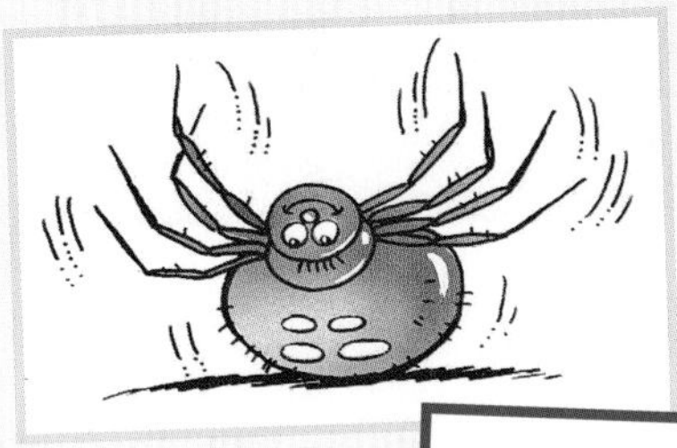

- **a** It's got four legs. ☐
- **b** Six legs. ☐
- **c** Eight legs. ☐

2 How much hair is there on this man's head?

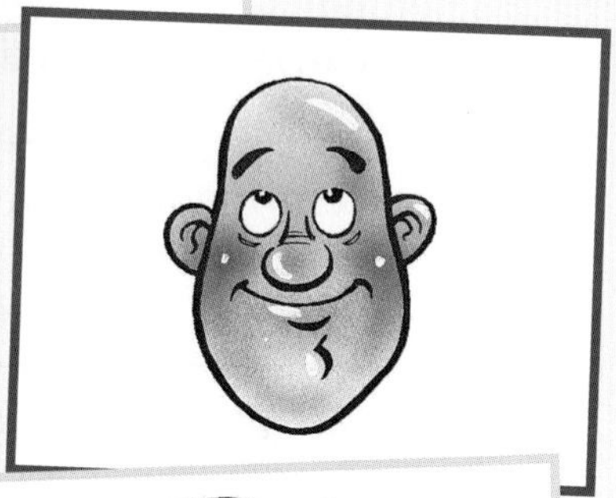

- **a** He hasn't got much hair. ☐
- **b** He hasn't got any hair. ☐
- **c** He's got some hair. ☐

3 A person has got two knees. How many knees has an elephant got?

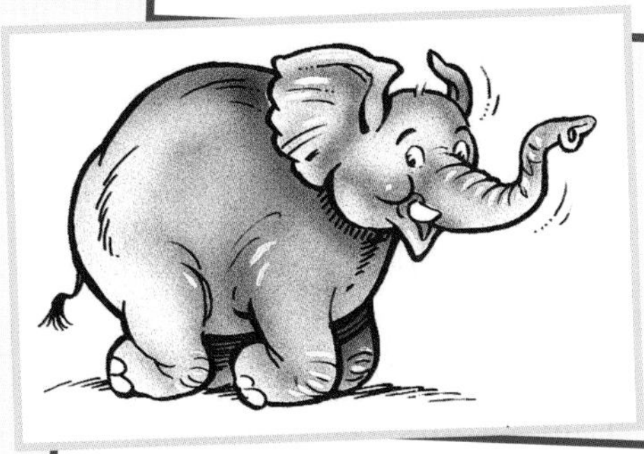

- **a** Don't be silly! An elephant hasn't got any knees. ☐
- **b** Two ☐
- **c** Four ☐

4 How much milk is there in the cat's bowl?

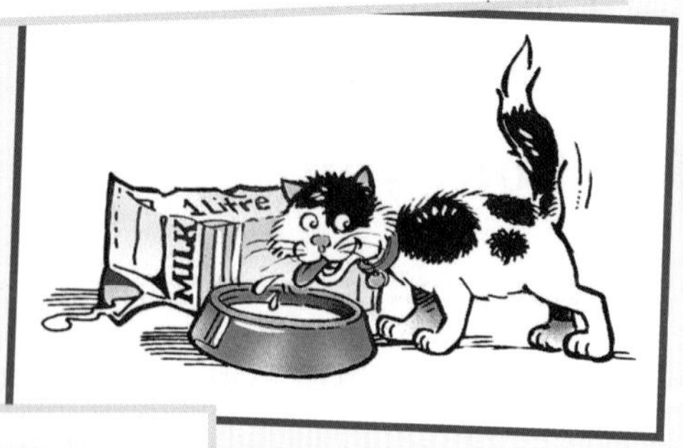

- **a** There isn't any milk. ☐
- **b** There isn't much milk. ☐
- **c** There's one litre. ☐

5 How many sides has a dice got?

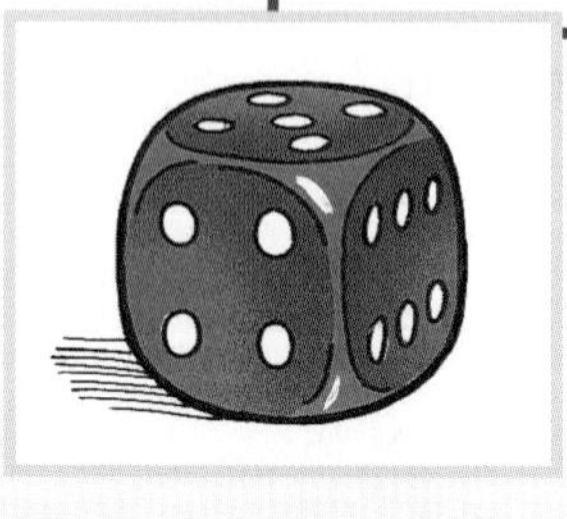

- **a** Not many – only four. ☐
- **b** It's got ten sides. ☐
- **c** Six sides. ☐

Answers: 1 c, 2 b, 3 c, 4 c, 5 c

How many? — not many			How much? — not much		
How many	bananas pens bicycles apples	are there? have we got?	How much	cheese water meat chocolate	is there? have we got?
There aren't We haven't got	many	eggs. sweets.	There isn't We haven't got	much	meat. lemonade.

1 We use **How many?** and **not many** with countable nouns, and **How much?** and **not much** with uncountable nouns (see Unit 9).

2 When we use **not many / not much**, the word **not** is usually part of the negative verb: **There are<u>n't</u> <u>many</u> dogs. / We have<u>n't</u> got <u>much</u> money.**

1   *Fill in the blanks with* How many *or* How much.

1 <u>How much</u>............ lemonade have we got? – Not much.

2 <u>How many</u>.......... bottles are there? – Three.

3 .... fruit is there? – We've got 6 apples and 2 oranges.

4 .... bananas have we got? – We haven't got any.

5 .... bread have we got? – Not much.

6 .... pens are there in your bag? – Six.

7 .... money have we got? – We haven't got much.

8 .... bicycles are there in the garden. – Two.

Partitives

Uncountables	Partitives	
water	a jug of water	2 glasses of water
lemonade	a bottle of lemonade	3 cans of lemonade
cheese	a piece of cheese	a kilo of cheese
meat	a piece of meat	a slice of meat
bread	a loaf of bread	2 slices of bread
chocolate	a piece of chocolate	a bar of chocolate
orange juice	a carton of orange juice	3 glasses of orange juice
coffee	a jug of coffee	4 cups of coffee
toothpaste	a tube of toothpaste	3 tubes of toothpaste

We can often express countable ideas with uncountable nouns by using the partitive **of** before the noun. We *can't* say **2 breads**, but we *can* say **2 loaves of bread**. And we *can't* say **4 waters**, but we *can* say **4 glasses of water**.

2 *Look at the pictures and say and write the descriptions.*

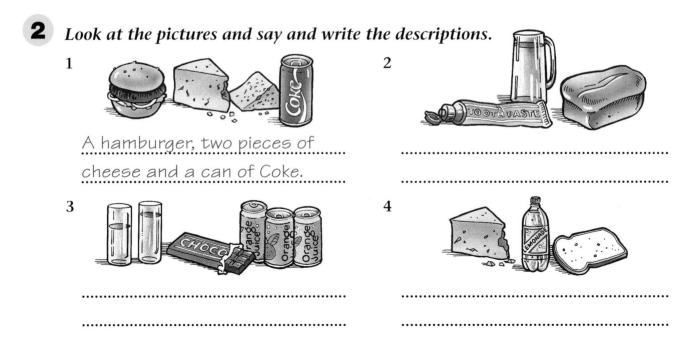

1   A hamburger, two pieces of
cheese and a can of Coke.

2   ....
....

3   ....
....

4   ....
....

3 *Ask and answer the questions. Then write the conversations.*

1 How much / bread / there / kitchen?
We / got / one loaf of bread / six rolls
A: How much bread is there in the kitchen?
B: We've got one loaf of bread and six rolls.

2 How much / toothpaste / we / got / bathroom?
There / two tubes of toothpaste
A: ....
B: ....

3 How much / lemonade / we / got / in / fridge?
We / got / one bottle of lemonade / four cans
A: ....
B: ....

4 *Write a silly quiz for your friends with* How many ...? *or* How much ...?
Use is there, are there, has ... got *or* have ... got. *Here are some ideas for four questions.*

Some ideas

holes / a piece of Swiss cheese?

hair / an elephant?

worms / a bad apple?

horns / a bull?

ANOTHER SILLY QUIZ

1 How many holes are there in a piece of Swiss cheese?
2 How much hair has an elephant got?
3 ....
4 ....
5 ....

15 can, can't

Captain Strong can!

Captain Strong can fly.

Bonjour! Guten Morgen! Buongiorno!

Captain Strong can speak 10 languages.

Look at Captain Strong's men. They can drive space cars.

Captain Strong can't ride this mountain bike. He's too big!

Affirmative	Negative	
	Full form	**Short form**
I can sing	I cannot sing	I can't sing
you can sing	you cannot sing	you can't sing
he can sing	he cannot sing	he can't sing
she can sing	she cannot sing	she can't sing
it can sing	it cannot sing	it can't sing
we can sing	we cannot sing	we can't sing
you can sing	you cannot sing	you can't sing
they can sing	they cannot sing	they can't sing

1 The verb **can** is followed by the base form of the verb, or the infinitive without **to**: **He can fly.** NOT ~~He can to fly~~.

2 We write the negative full form **cannot** as one word with two **nn**s; we write the short form **can't** with one **n**.

1 *Fill in the blanks with* can *or* can't.

Captain Strong (1)...can.... fly, but he (2).............. ride a mountain bike.

He (3) .... speak ten languages. His men (4).............. drive space cars, but I

(5).............. drive a space car. I (6).............. ride a bicycle, but I (7).............. fly and I

(8)............ speak ten languages.

Interrogative	Short answers	
	Affirmative	**Negative**
can I sing?	Yes, I can.	No, I can't.
can you sing?	Yes, you can.	No, you can't.
can he sing?	Yes, he can.	No, he can't.
can she sing?	Yes, she can.	No, she can't.
can it sing?	Yes, it can.	No, it can't.
can we sing?	Yes, we can.	No, we can't.
can you sing?	Yes, you can.	No, you can't.
can they sing?	Yes, they can.	No, they can't.

With **Yes / No** short answers, we use the verb **can / can't** and leave out the main verb and the rest of the sentence.

2 *Ask and answer the questions. Then write the short answers.*

1 Can Captain Strong fly?   Yes, he can.
2 Can he ride a mountain bike? No, ...
3 Can Scamp and Mog cook?   No, ...
4 Can Mum play tennis?   Yes, ...

5 Can John and Jane swim?   Yes, ...
6 Can Liz speak Greek?   No, ...
7 Can Mary sing? No, ...
8 Can *you* swim? ....

3 *Make the questions. Then write them.*

1   Captain Strong   can   10 languages   speak   ?

   Can Captain Strong speak 10 languages?

2   English   Mog   speak   can   ?

   ....

3   Liz and Jane   swim   can   ?

   ....

4   John   can   tennis   play   ?

   ....

5   you   English   understand   can   ?

   ....

What	can I see?
	can you see?
	can he see?
Who	can she see?
	can it see?
How many	can we see?
	can you see?
	can they see?

4 *How many of these can you see in the picture – mice, cats, babies, policemen, bicycles, birds, dogs, cameras, pianos, sunglasses? Say and write the sentences.*

I can see four mice. ....

....

But I can't see any ....

....

5 *Make ten true sentences, then write them.*
Use can *five times, and use* can't *five times.*

Fish		climb trees.
Penguins	can	fly.
Dogs		sing.
Birds		swim.
Some parrots	can't	talk.
Cats		run fast.

4 ....

5 ....

6 ....

7 ....

1 *Dogs can't sing.*

8 ....

2 *Cats can run fast.*

9 ....

3 ....

10 ....

6 **About you**

Look at these words.

sing	swim	run fast	cook	type	draw	paint

play	{ tennis football the piano the guitar	speak	{ English Greek Italian German	ride	{ a bike a horse a motorbike an elephant	use	{ a camera a computer a calculator a microwave

What can you do? What can't you do? Write full sentences, as in the examples.

I can swim, but I can't type. I can play tennis, but I can't ride a horse.

....

....

....

....

And your family and friends? What can they do? What can't they do?

My brother can speak English, but he can't speak Italian. My friends

Jane and John can use a computer, but they can't use calculators.

....

....

....

16 Object pronouns *me*, *you*, *him*, etc.

Look at me!

Ooh! Look at me!

It's a ghost. Listen to it! Call Mum and Dad! Call them!

Don't be silly! It's Liz under a sheet. You can't see her, but she can see you.

Subject pronouns	Object pronouns	
I	me	Listen to **me**.
you	you	I can see **you**.
he	him	Can you find **him**?
she	her	Look at **her**.
it	it	Can you paint **it**?
we	us	Can you play with **us**?
you	you	We can see **you**.
they	them	Can you draw **them**?

1 *Fill in the blanks with the correct object pronouns.*

1 Look at ..me.. ! I'm a ghost.

2 Look at that ghost! Listen to .... !

3 Call Mum and Dad. Call .... !

4 I'm a ghost. You can't see ...., but I can see ....

5 It's Liz. She can see ...., but you can't see ....

2 *Say the sentences. Fill in the blanks with these words.*

1 There's a man over there. Can you see ..him. ?

2 There's Jane's mum. Can you see .... ?

3 There are two men in the park. Can you see .... ?

4 We are in the garden. Can you see .... ?

them   us
her   him ✔

3 *Rewrite these sentences.*

1 Watch <u>the children</u>.

  Watch them. ....

2 Don't eat <u>the apple</u>.

  ....

3 Look at <u>the man</u>.

  ....

4 Ask <u>Mary</u> about her school.

  ....

5 <u>I</u> want John's address.

  Give ....

6 Can you phone <u>John and me</u>?

  ....

4 *Complete this table.*

Subject pronouns	I	you	he	she	....	we	....	they
Object pronouns	me	....	....	her	it	....	you	them
Possessive adjectives	my	your	his	....	....	our	....	....
Possessive pronouns	mine	....	....	....	its	....	yours	....

Now fill in the blanks with words from the table.

1

I'm Mog. Can you see ...me...?
This is my fish. And those
mice are mine, too.

2

This is Liz.
This is ....
favourite toy.
And these toys
are .... ,
too.

3

That's Scamp. Can you see
.... ? This is .... collar.
And that bone is ....

4

Here are Mum
and Dad. You
can see ....
This is ....
house. And this
car is ....

17 Present simple (1)

Mog gets up late every day

You have a boring life, Mog.

Yes, I *am* bored! I *do* the same things every day.

What *do* you *do*? You don't read comics, you don't play the piano, you don't help people, you don't watch TV, ...

I get up late every morning and go for a walk in the garden. Then I have breakfast and sleep. Then I have lunch and sleep again.

What *does* that cat *do* all day? He doesn't do much.

No, I don't do much. But I catch mice!

Affirmative	Negative	
	Full form	**Short form**
I read	I do not read	I don't read
you read	you do not read	you don't read
he reads	he does not read	he doesn't read
she reads	she does not read	she doesn't read
it reads	it does not read	it doesn't read
we read	we do not read	we don't read
you read	you do not read	you don't read
they read	they do not read	they don't read

1 The Present simple is used to describe actions that we do regularly or do every day: **I get up late every morning. / He does the same things every day.**

2 We use the base form of the verb with **I, you, we** and **they**: We <u>read</u> comics. We add an **s** to the verb with 3rd person singular **he, she** and **it**: She <u>reads</u> comics.

3 We add **do not / don't** to the base verb to form the negative for **I, you, we, they: I <u>don't eat</u> fish.** We add **does not / doesn't** to the base verb to form the negative with **he, she, it: He <u>doesn't eat</u> meat.**

4 In a sentence like **He doesn't do much all day**, the verb **do** is both an auxiliary (or helper) verb (**doesn't**) *and* a full verb (**do**).

1 *Say these sentences with the correct form of the verbs in brackets. Then write them.*

1 Mog <u>.gets up..</u> late every morning. (get up)

2 He .... after breakfast. (sleep)

3 He .... TV. (not / watch)

4 He .... comics. (not / read)

5 He .... the piano. (not / play)

6 He .... mice. (catch)

2 *Say and write the correct form of the verbs* play, watch *or* read.

1 I ...read... a comic every day.   4 He .... TV every afternoon.

2 She .... a magazine every day.   5 They .... chess every evening.

3 We .... TV every evening.   6 He .... computer games every evening.

With the third person singular, is it **s**, **es**, or **ies**? Look at this.

1 We add **s** to the base verb form with verbs like **drink, run, speak, visit, wear > He drinks, runs, speaks, visits, wears**

2 We add **s** to words like these that end in **e: come, give, hate, like, live, make > He comes, gives, hates, likes, lives, makes**

3 We add **es** to words that end in **ch, sh, ss, x, o: brush, do, dress, go, mix, polish, teach, wash, watch > He brushes, does, dresses, goes, mixes, polishes, teaches, washes, watches**

4 With verbs that end in **y**, we change the **y** to **ies: cry, fly, try > He cries, flies, tries** But notice these: **buy > buys, play > plays, say > says**

3 *Say the sentences with* he *or* she. *Then write them.*

1 I speak English.   She speaks English.

2 I brush my teeth.   ....

3 You cry all the time.   ....

4 They hate coffee.   ....

5 They play football.   ....

6 I wear glasses.   ....

7 We live in a town.   ....

8 I go to the beach.   ....

9 They wash after breakfast.   ....

10 We get up late.   ....

Interrogative	Short Answers	
	Affirmative	Negative
do I read?	Yes, I do.	No, I don't.
do you read?	Yes, you do.	No, you don't.
does he read?	Yes, he does.	No, he doesn't.
does she read?	Yes, she does.	No, she doesn't.
does it read?	Yes, it does.	No, it doesn't.
do we read?	Yes, we do.	No, we don't.
do you read?	Yes, you do.	No, you don't.
do they read?	Yes, they do.	No, they don't.

1 We form present simple questions and short answers with the auxiliary verb **do / does: Does Mog catch mice? Yes, he does. / No, he doesn't.**

4 *Ask and answer questions from the prompts. Then write them.*

1 she / read / many books? Yes .....*Does she read many books? Yes, she does.*.....

2 you / eat / many vegetables? No ....

3 he / teach / English? No ....

Do you **ever** go to the cinema?	No, I **never** go to the cinema.

How often do you go to the cinema?	Oh, I always / often / sometimes / usually go to the cinema on Saturdays.

Frequency adverbs (**always, often, sometimes,** etc.) are placed before the main verb in affirmatives, negatives and questions: **He <u>usually comes</u> here after lunch. / I don't <u>often visit</u> them. / Do you <u>always go</u> there?**

5 *What does Scamp do every day? What do you think?*
Use never, always, often, sometimes *or* usually.
Say and write sentences.

1 get up / 6 o'clock   <u>He always gets up at 6 o'clock.</u>

2 go for a walk / 6.30   ....

3 breakfast / 8 o'clock ....

4 lunch / 12 o'clock   ....

5 sleep / after lunch   ....

6 *What does Scamp do every day? What do you think?*
Make the questions and then answer them.

1 always / get up / early?   <u>Does Scamp always get up early?</u>...................
                             <u>– Yes, he does.</u>...

2 often / go / for a walk?   ....
                             ....

3 ever / have breakfast early? ....
                             ....

4 always / have lunch?   ....
                             ....

5 ever / sleep after lunch? ....
                             ....

7 *Do this puzzle. Then look at the*
column down and answer the question.

1 He doesn't speak French.
  He ... English.
2 He doesn't wear new clothes.
  He ... old clothes.
3 He doesn't often visit Paris.
  He often ... Athens.
4 He doesn't drink tea. He ...
  coffee.
5 He doesn't work in an office.
  He ... in his studio.
6 He doesn't eat meat. He ... fish.

What does he do? – He's an ....

18 Present continuous

We are sitting in a Jumbo Jet

JOHN: What are you doing, Liz?
LIZ: I'm reading a postcard from Mike.
JOHN: Where's it from? Where is he?
JANE: Read it to us!
LIZ: Oh, all right.

Dear Liz, John and Jane,
We are sitting in a Jumbo Jet 35,000 feet over the Atlantic. We are flying to America and having a meal. We're going to Florida for our holiday. Just think–Disney World, Universal Studios and Sea World! My dad's bored. He's reading a newspaper! Best wishes and see you all soon, Mike

ORLANDO. FL 328 PM 08 OCT

USA 29

The Baker 'kids',
4, The Avenue,
The Village,
High Town,
Countyshire,
England

Affirmative		Negative	
Full form	**Short form**	**Full form**	**Short form**
I am eating	I'm eating	I am not eating	I'm not eating
you are eating	you're eating	you are not eating	you aren't eating
he is eating	he's eating	he is not eating	he isn't eating
she is eating	she's eating	she is not eating	she isn't eating
it is eating	it's eating	it is not eating	it isn't eating
we are eating	we're eating	we are not eating	we aren't eating
you are eating	you're eating	you are not eating	you aren't eating
they are eating	they're eating	they are not eating	they aren't eating

1 We form the Present continuous with the present of the verb **be** + the present participle of the verb (**eating, flying, reading**, etc.): **We are flying**

2 We use the Present continuous for an action which is happening now, the moment we are speaking.

1 *Complete these sentences about Mike and his family.*

1 Mike .is sitting. in a Jumbo Jet. (sit)

2 He and his family .... to America. (fly)

3 They .... a meal. (have)

4 They .... to Florida for their holiday. (go)

5 Mike's dad .... a newspaper. (read)

2 *Look at the pictures. Say and write sentences. Use short forms.*

1

She's eating an apple. ....

She isn't eating cherries. ....

2

They ....

....

3

I ....

....

4

He ....

....

5

We ....

....

6

....

....

> What are you doing at the moment, Captain Strong? Are you reading?

> Yes, I'm studying present continuous spelling! Look!

Present continuous spelling

1 We usually add **-ing** to the verb:
   *do — do**ing**, read — read**ing**, fly — fly**ing**, eat — eat**ing***

2 If a verb ends with an **e**, we take away the **e** and add **-ing**:
   *have — hav**ing**, ride — rid**ing**, write — writ**ing***
   But look, **ie** changes to **y** + **-ing** : *lie — l**ying***

3 If a verb has a short vowel and one consonant, we double the consonant and add
   -ing: *sit — si**tt**ing, run — ru**nn**ing, swim — swi**mm**ing.*

3 ***What are they doing** at the moment? Say these sentences with the –ing form.
   Then write them.*

1 She's ....playing......... . (play)

2 They're .... (paint)

3 I'm not .... lunch. (have)

4 He isn't .... (swim)

5 She's .... (read)

6 He's .... his bike. (ride)

7 We aren't .... (run)

8 They're .... in Dad's car. (sit)

9 She's .... (draw)

10 I'm .... a postcard. (write)

Interrogative	Short answers	
	Affirmative	**Negative**
am I eating?	Yes, I am.	No, I'm not.
are you eating?	Yes, you are.	No, you aren't.
is he eating?	Yes, he is.	No, he isn't.
is she eating?	Yes, she is.	No, she isn't.
is it eating?	Yes, it is.	No, it isn't.
are we eating?	Yes, we are.	No, we aren't.
are you eating?	Yes, you are.	No, you aren't.
are they eating?	Yes, they are.	No, they aren't.

> Jane, are you eating?

> No, I'm not.

> Yes, you are.

In short **Yes / No** answers to questions, we use the verb **be** and leave out the rest of the sentence: **Are you eating? Yes, I am. / No, I'm not.**

4 *Ask and answer the questions. Then write them.*

1 you / read / a book? – No / I / read / a magazine.
   Are you reading a book? – No, I'm not. I'm reading a magazine.

2 she / wash / glasses? – No / she / wash / cups and saucers.

   ....

3 they / write / postcards? – No / they / write / letters.

   ....

4 Captain Strong / fly / to the moon? – No / he / fly / to America.

   ....

5 you two / play / chess? – No / we / play / Monopoly.

   ....

5 *Match the questions and answers. Then say them with a partner.*

1 What are you reading?   a They're eating a pizza.

2 Where is he sitting?   b She's talking to John Brown.

3 Who is she talking to?   c I'm waiting for our teacher.

4 What are you doing here?   d I'm reading a comic.

5 What are they eating?   e He's sitting in the corner.

6 **About you**

Find photos of you and your family, your friends, your animals, etc. Stick them on paper, or draw pictures.

This is me. I'm sitting on the beach and I'm reading a book.

Then write under them, like this:

Present simple (2) – time prepositions

Silly questions

JOHN: Mike always watches football on TV on Mondays in winter.

DAD: Oh, does he?

JANE: Yes, and he and his sisters usually watch the late night film on Thursdays.

DAD: Do they?

LIZ: Yes, and Mike often goes to the cinema on Wednesdays.

DAD: Does he? And when does Mike do his homework?

LIZ: Oh, Dad. Why do you always ask silly questions?

What time do you get up?	— **At** 6 o'clock. / **At** half past eight.
When do you get up?	— **At** 7 o'clock. / **At** half past seven.
When do you go skiing?	— **In** January. / **In** February. / **In** March. / **In** April. *
When does it rain here?	— **In** autumn. / **In** winter. / **In** spring. / **In** summer.
When does she go to town?	— **On** Mondays. / **Every** Monday.
When does he play football?	— **On** Tuesday mornings. / **Every** Tuesday morning.
When do they play golf?	— **On** Friday afternoons. / **Every** Friday afternoon.
When do you watch football?	— **On** Thursday evenings. / **Every** Thursday evening. / **In** the evening.

* January, February, March, April, May, June, July,
August, September, October, November, December

We use: **at** with times (**at 9 o'clock**),
in with seasons and months (**in winter, in July**),
on with days of the week (**on Saturdays**), and parts of days
(**on Sunday afternoons**).
Note the **s** on days and parts of days to show regularity.

1 *Correct these sentences about Mike and his sisters.*

1 Mike always watches football on Saturdays in summer.
   No, he doesn't. He always watches football on Mondays in winter.

2 Mike and his sisters watch the late night film on Sundays.

   ....

   ....

3 Mike always goes to the cinema on Wednesdays.

   ....

   ....

2 *This is a typical week for the Baker family.*
Ask and answer the questions. Then write the answers.

	MORNING	AFTERNOON	EVENING
Monday	Mum and Dad go to work.		John plays basketball.
Tuesday		Liz takes Scamp for a walk.	
Wednesday	Mog watches TV.		Dad and John watch football.
Thursday			Jane does her homework.
Friday		Liz and Jane play tennis.	Mum cooks a special meal.

1 What do Mum and Dad always do on Monday mornings?
   They always go to work.

2 What does Liz sometimes do on Tuesday afternoons?

   ....

3 What does John usually do on Monday evenings?

   ....

4 What does Jane usually do on Thursday evenings?

   ....

5 What do Liz and Jane sometimes do on Friday afternoons?

   ....

3 *Put these words and phrases in the correct columns below.*

March ✔   Mondays ✔   8.30 ✔   Thursday afternoons   12.00

August   Tuesday evenings   3 o'clock   Wednesdays   2.15

winter   spring   the evening   6.45   Saturday mornings

at	in	on
8.30	March	Mondays
....	....	....
....	....	....
....	....	....
....	....	....

4 *Say these sentences with* in, at *or* on. *Then write in the words.*

1 He's usually here ..at.. 4 o'clock.

2 I'm always here .... the afternoons.

3 My birthday's .... March.

4 It often snows .... winter.

5 That programme always starts
    .... 7 o'clock.

6 What do you do .... Tuesday evenings?

7 He's never here .... Mondays.

8 It's often wet there .... August.

9 The film starts .... 7.30 every evening.

10 It's always hot here .... summer.

5   *Write conversations about the pictures.*

1

often / Saturdays

A: Does.. John ever play football?

B: Yes, he does.

   He often plays football.

A: When?

B: On Saturdays.

2

always / Monday evenings

A: .... Liz ....

B: ....

   ....

A: ....

B: ....

3

often / Thursday afternoons

A: .... the children ....

B: ....

   ....

A: ....

B: ....

4

often / Saturday evenings

A: .... Dad ....

B: ....

   ....

A: ....

B: ....

6   **About you**

Write what you and your family **always/usually/often/sometimes/never** *do.*

1 I (or we) usually get up early .... on Monday mornings.

2 .... in July.

3 .... on Saturday evenings.

4 .... in winter.

5 .... at 7.00 on Saturday mornings.

6 .... on Sundays in summer.

20 Present simple (3) with *come from*, *like*, etc.

I hate spiders

John is interviewing Jo Grey.
She is a pop singer.

JOHN: Miss Grey, where do
you come from?

JO: I come from England.

JOHN: And where do you live?

JO: I live in London.

JOHN: What languages do you
speak?

JO: English, of course.
And I speak French and
Spanish, too.

JOHN: What food do you like?

JO: Oh, Italian food.
I love Italian food.

JOHN: What do you hate?

JO: What do I hate? I hate
spiders!

JOHN: Do you know any
famous people,
Miss Grey?

JO: Yes, of course I do.
I know Madonna.

JOHN: Wow!

We always use the simple tense form with the verbs in these sentences.

He **comes from** Italy.	Do you **know** Liz and Jane?
She **likes** pop music.	I **believe** you.
They **love** ice cream.	She **hates** cockroaches.
He **needs** a new book.	I **want** some new shoes.
What does that word **mean**?	I **remember** that day very well.
This car **belongs** to me.	He **owns** a big house.

We also usually use the simple form of verbs like **live** and **speak** when talking about permanent situations, general actions or truths:

She **lives** in London.   She **speaks** English.

1 All the verbs above are rarely used in the continuous form.

2 Remember too that the verb **have** (= **own, possess**) is also only used in the simple form, *and* the verb **do** when asking about professions or jobs: **What do you do? — I'm an engineer.**

1 *Here are some sentences about Liz. Fill in the blanks with the correct form of these verbs.*

hate	like	speak	come from ✔	live	have

1 Liz <u>comes from</u> England.

2 She .... near London.

3 She .... English.

4 She .... a cat and a dog.

5 She .... television.

6 She .... homework.

2 *Write a paragraph about the singer Jo Grey for a magazine.*

1 What does Jo Grey do?

2 Where does she come from?

3 Where does she live?

4 What languages does she speak?

5 What food does she like?

6 What does she hate?

7 Does she know any famous people?

Jo Grey — pop singer

Jo Grey ....

and she ....

She ....

She ....

....

She ....

but she ....

She ....

3 *Match the questions and answers.*

1 Do you know that man?

2 What's his name?

3 What does he do?

4 What does he want?

5 What language does he speak?

6 Where does he come from?

7 Where does he live?

8 What time does he get up?

9 Do you know his address?

a Italy.

b Sergio.

c Italian.

d Yes, I do.

e In Rome.

f At 6 o'clock.

g A new car.

h He's a waiter.

i Yes, it's 50, The Avenue.

4 ***What do you know about wild animals?***
Answer the questions in this quiz.

1 Where do giraffes come from?

  a Asia   **b** Africa   **c** America

2 What food do giraffes like?

  a Leaves   **b** Meat   **c** Fish

3 What do giraffes have?

  a Short legs   **b** A long neck   **c** Three stomachs

4 Where do leopards live?

  a Australia   **b** Africa   **c** America

5 What food do leopards like?

  a Meat   **b** Grass   **c** Leaves

6 What colour fur do leopards have?

  a White or cream with small black circles

  b Black with white stripes

  c Yellow with black spots

7 Where do kangaroos come from?

  a Europe   **b** America   **c** Australia

8 What do kangaroos eat?

  a Mice   **b** Grass   **c** Vegetables

9 Where do kangaroos carry their babies?

  a On their back   **b** Under their arm

  c In a pouch

5 ***Now write about giraffes, leopards and kangaroos.***

1 Giraffes are very tall. They come from Africa. ....

  ....

2 Leopards are 'big cats'. ....

  ....

3 Kangaroos come ....

  ....

Answers: 1b, 2a, 3b, 4b, 5a, 6a, 7c, 8b, 9c.

6 *Look at this picture. Read his answers and then write the questions.*

1 What / name?

~~What is your name?~~

2 Where / come from?

....

3 What language / speak?

....

4 How / breathe?

....

5 What / eat / drink?

....

6 What / drive?

....

7 What / want here?

....

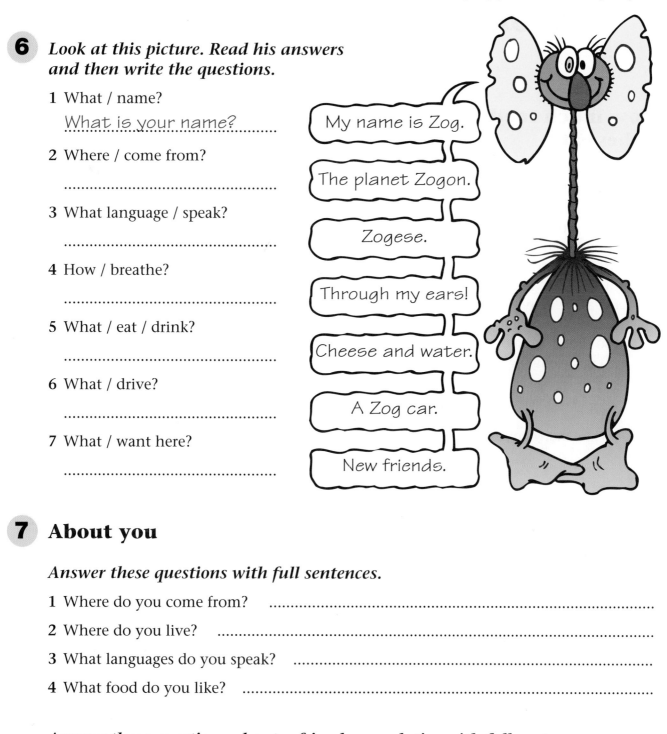

My name is Zog.

The planet Zogon.

Zogese.

Through my ears!

Cheese and water.

A Zog car.

New friends.

7 ## About you

Answer these questions with full sentences.

1 Where do you come from? ....

2 Where do you live? ....

3 What languages do you speak? ....

4 What food do you like? ....

Answer these questions about a friend or a relative with full sentences.

1 What is your friend's / relative's name?   My ....

2 Where does he / she come from? ....

3 Where does he / she live? ....

4 What languages does he / she speak? ....

5 What food does he / she like? ....

6 What food or drink *doesn't* he / she like? ....

21 Quantity: *too many, too much, a lot (of), a few, a little, not enough*

How much food do fishes eat?

JANE: Dad, what do fishes eat?

DAD: Special fish food. And you only give them food once a day – but not too much.

JANE: How much food do fishes eat, then?

DAD: Just a little. They don't eat a lot. Why?

JANE: I think I give ours too much. One of them's *really* big!

Well, they *don't* give me too much! In fact, they don't give me enough food. Just look at me. I'm so thin!

How many comics have they got?

Not many.
Not many comics.

Too many.
Too many comics.

A lot.
A lot of comics.

How much ice cream have they got?

Not much.
Not much ice cream.

Too much.
Too much ice cream.

A lot.
A lot of ice cream.

We can use **a lot of** and **a lot** with countable *and* uncountable nouns.

A lot can be used on its own: **How much ice cream does she eat? — A lot. / How many people do you know? — A lot.**

A lot of *must* be followed by a noun or pronoun: **She eats a lot of ice cream. / I know a lot of people. / The children read a lot of them.**

1 *Fill in the blanks with* **How many, How much, too many** *or* **too much.**

1 ...How much... special food do you give fishes?

   – I don't know, but don't give them ....

2 .... fishes has Jane got? – I can see four.

3 .... food does Jane give to her fishes? – She gives them .... !

4 Do they give Mog .... food? – I don't know, but he eats

   .... hamburgers!

2 *The Bakers are having a picnic. Who is saying what? Read these sentences.*
Then write them in the correct speech bubbles.

- How much ice cream do you want?
- This is too much meat for me. I can't eat it.
- There are too many crisps for me.
- There's a lot of orange juice.
- How many sandwiches do you want? ✔
- Come on, have a cake. There are a lot here.

1 How many sandwiches do you want?

2 ....

3 ....

4 ....

5 ....

6 ....

a few	sweets / chips / vegetables / herbs	....
		....
a little	food / water / sugar / salt / oil / pepper	....
		....
not enough	sweets / vegetables / chips	....
		....
	food / water / salt / sugar / oil / pepper	....
		....

We use **a few** only with countable nouns: **I've got a few friends.**

We use **a little** only with uncountable nouns: **Just a little milk, please.**

We can use **not enough** with countable and uncountable nouns: **I haven't got enough money. / There aren't enough sandwiches.**

3 *Choose some of these words and write them in the correct spaces in the box above.*

fruit	cherries	ice cream	books	snow	coffee	comics	apples
hair	chocolate	sandwiches	shoes	milk	hamburgers	bananas
		oranges	stamps	tomato ketchup		

4 *Put these phrases in the correct sentences.*

> not enough sugar   a few English students   too many sweets   a lot of vegetables
> too much salt ✔   a little toothpaste   not many rhinos   a few chips

1 There is ...*too much salt*............. in this soup. It's horrible!

2 We eat .... in our house because they are good for you.

3 There are .... in our school. They all come from London.

4 There are .... in the world. There are some in Africa and
there are a lot in zoos.

5 You eat .... They're not good for your teeth.

6 There is .... in this pudding. I like sweet puddings.

7 Can I have just .... with my fish, please? I can't eat many.

8 You only need .... to clean your teeth. You don't need a lot.

5 **About you**

Answer these questions with full sentences.

1 What food do you like?   ....
....

2 Do you eat a lot of these?   ....
  – meat? eggs? sweets? biscuits?   ....
  hamburgers? chocolate?   ....

3 How much fruit and how   ....
  many vegetables do you eat   ....
  every day? (a lot? not much?   ....
  not many?)   ....

4 How many of these do you eat   ....
  in a week? – bananas? apples?   ....
  oranges?   ....

5 What do you drink? Do you   ....
  drink much coke? milk? water?   ....

22 Simple past of verb *be*

Captain Strong was there

Where were you yesterday, Captain Strong?

I was in the Sahara Desert. It was hot!

Were you on the Moon last week?

No, I wasn't. I was at the Pyramids in Egypt. It was very hot there.

Were you and your men on Earth last year?

No, we weren't. We were on Mercury. It was very hot there as well.

And where were you last month?

Last month? I was on holiday on Mars. It was quite cool there.

Affirmative	Negative	
	Full form	**Short form**
I was	I was not	I wasn't
you were	you were not	you weren't
he was	he was not	he wasn't
she was	she was not	she wasn't
it was	it was not	it wasn't
we were	we were not	we weren't
you were	you were not	you weren't
they were	they were not	they weren't

1 The simple past of the verb **be** is **was / were: I/he/she/it was/wasn't, we/you/they were/weren't.**

2 We often use it with words and phrases like **yesterday, last week, last month, last year.**

3 We use **It was ...** (+ adjective) to describe the weather in the past: **It was hot yesterday.**

1 *This is about Captain Strong and his men.*
Fill in the blanks with **was, wasn't, were** *or* **weren't.**

Captain Strong (1) wasn't at home yesterday. He (2).............. in the Sahara Desert.

It (3).............. hot there. And Captain Strong (4).............. on the Moon last week.

He (5).............. at the Pyramids in Egypt. It (6).............. very hot there. Last year

Captain Strong and his men (7).............. on Earth. They (8).............. on Mercury.

It (9).............. very hot there as well. And last month? Where (10)..............

Captain Strong last month? He (11).............. on holiday on Mars. It (12)..............

quite cool there. It (13).............. hot.

> Was Jane really ill yesterday?

> Yes, she was.

> No, she wasn't!

Interrogative	Short answers	
	Affirmative	**Negative**
was I?	Yes, I was.	No, I wasn't.
were you?	Yes, you were.	No, you weren't.
was he?	Yes, he was.	No, he wasn't.
was she?	Yes, she was.	No, she wasn't.
was it?	Yes, it was.	No, it wasn't.
were we?	Yes, we were.	No, we weren't.
were you?	Yes, you were.	No, you weren't.
were they?	Yes, they were.	No, they weren't.

In short **Yes / No** answers we simply use **was / were** and leave out the rest of the sentence: **Were you at school yesterday? — Yes, I was. / No, I wasn't.**

2 *Ask and answer questions about Captain Strong and his men.*
Then write the short answers.

1 Was Captain Strong in the Sahara yesterday?   Yes, he was.

2 Was he on the Moon last week?   ....

3 Was he at the Pyramids in Egypt?   ....

4 Were he and his men on Earth last year?   ....

5 Were they on Mercury then?   ....

6 Was Captain Strong on Mars last month?   ....

7 Was it hot there?   ....

8 Was it quite cool there?   ....

I **was** there	yesterday	**at** 6 o'clock.
I **wasn't** there	last week	**at** half past eight.
We **were** there	last weekend	**at** the weekend.
We **weren't** there	last Monday	**on** Monday.
	last month	**last** March / **in** March.
	last year	**in** 1995.

3 *Join these words and phrases to make sentences with* was *or* were.
There are no right and wrong answers.

John	in London	yesterday.
Mog	at school	last Saturday.
Jane	at work	last week.
Scamp	in town	last month.
Mum and Dad	in hospital	last year.
It / hot	at home	last July.

1 *Scamp was at home yesterday.* ....

2 ....

3 ....

4 ....

5 ....

6 ....

4 *Re-order these words to make sentences or questions. Begin with the underlined words. Then write all the last letters in the column to make the name of a place in America.*

1	good	weather	was	The			The weather was good......	.D..
2	spaghetti	you	Do	like	?		....	....
3	Mars	Captain	was	on	Strong		....	....
4	London	He	in	lives			....	....
5	here	rains	It	often			....	....
6	you	Where	yesterday	were	?		....	....
7	shop window	It	in	was	the		....	....
8	listening	you	What	are	to	?	....	....
9	summer	We	Greece	in	were	last	....	....
							....	....
10	cool	was	quite	it	Last week		....	....
11	last weekend	Athens	in	was	I		....	....

The place is ....

5 **About you**

Answer these questions with full sentences.

1 Where were you last Saturday? ....

2 Who were you with? ....

3 What was the weather like? ....

4 And where were you last Sunday? ....

5 Who was there with you? ....

6 What was the weather like? ....

23 Simple past of verb *have*

We had a day out

JASON: Where were you yesterday?

JANE: We had a day out with Dad. We were at the funfair.

LIZ: Yes, there are lots of things there – the Octopus, the Big Dipper …

JASON: Did you have a good time?

JOHN: Yes! We had a ride on the Big Dipper.

LIZ: Jane didn't. She's too young.

JANE: But I had a ride on the Roundabout – and we had hamburgers and coke for lunch.

JOHN: And we all had ice creams!

LIZ: We didn't have any sweets, but we had a fantastic day.

DAD: At the end of the day I had a headache – and I didn't have any money!

JANE: Poor Dad!

Affirmative	Negative	
	Full form	**Short form**
I had	I did not have	I didn't have
you had	you did not have	you didn't have
he had	he did not have	he didn't have
she had	she did not have	she didn't have
it had	it did not have	it didn't have
we had	we did not have	we didn't have
you had	you did not have	you didn't have
they had	they did not have	they didn't have

1 The simple past affirmative of the verb **have** is **had** for all persons.

2 We form the negative with the simple past **did not / didn't** of the helper verb **do**: **She did not have a good time. / I didn't have any money.**

1 *Liz wrote this letter to a friend. Fill in the blanks with* **had** *or* **didn't have.**

Yesterday we (1)......had...... a day out at the funfair with Dad. We (2)................ a great day. Jane (3)................ a ride on the Big Dipper or the Octopus, but she (4)................ a ride on the roundabout. We (5)................ hamburgers and coke and ice creams, but we (6).......... .... any sweets.
At the end of the day Dad (7)................ a headache, and he (8)................ any money!

Did you have a good time here at home?

Yes, we did. It was very quiet.

No, we didn't! It was boring.

Interrogative	Short answers	
	Affirmative	**Negative**
did I have?	Yes, I did.	No, I didn't.
did you have?	Yes, you did.	No, you didn't.
did he have?	Yes, he did.	No, he didn't.
did she have?	Yes, she did.	No, she didn't.
did it have?	Yes, it did.	No, it didn't.
did we have?	Yes, we did.	No, we didn't.
did you have?	Yes, you did.	No, you didn't.
did they have?	Yes, they did.	No, they didn't.

In short **Yes / No** answers, we use the verb **did / didn't** and leave out the rest of the sentence: **Did you have hamburgers? Yes, we did. / No, we didn't.**

2 *Ask questions and give short answers. Then write them.*

1 the children / a day out with Dad yesterday? Did the children have a day out with Dad yesterday? – Yes, they did.

2 the children / a good time at the funfair? ....
....

3 Jane / a ride on the Big Dipper? ....
....

4 they / hamburgers and coke for lunch? ....
....

5 Dad / any money at the end of the day? ....
....

	a cold	now.
I've got	a headache	at the moment.
	a stomachache	today.
	toothache	
	flu	last Saturday.
I had	a broken arm	last week.
		last month.

With expressions to do with having illnesses like this, we usually use **has got / have got** (*not* simply **has / have**) in the present, and **had / didn't have** in the past.

3 *The Bakers are in a restaurant. Who says what?*
Read these sentences, then complete the conversation.

- And what did you have, Sue?
- I had a hamburger, Dad.
- What did you have? ✔

- I had chicken sandwiches.
- I just had a salad.
- And Liz and I had burgers, too, I know.

DAD: Waiter! Can we pay now?

WAITER: Of course, sir. (1) _What did you have?_ ....

JANE: (2) ....

DAD: (3) ....

So that's three hamburgers.

(4) ....

MUM: (5) ....

DAD: So you just had a salad.

JOHN: (6) ....

DAD: Chicken sandwiches. Oh, yes.

WAITER: Is that all? Good. Three hamburgers, chicken sandwiches, and a salad.

4 *Look at the pictures. Then say and write sentences.*

1 last week   this week

He had toothache last week, but he hasn't got toothache this week.

2 yesterday   today

She didn't have a headache yesterday, but she's got a headache today.

3 last month   this month

....
....
....
....

4 yesterday   today

....
....
....
....

5 last weekend   this weekend

....
....
....
....

6 yesterday   today

....
....
....
....

24 Simple past with regular verbs (and *ago*)

I dropped the camera!

Last Saturday I visited the Bakers.
That was a week ago. We had a great time.
Did we watch television? No, we didn't.
So what did we do?

First I played tennis with Mum. But it
rained, so the photo isn't very good.

Then I played football with Dad and John.
But they didn't stay still, so the photo
isn't very good.

Later, Liz and Jane tidied their rooms.
I dropped the camera, so the photo
isn't very good!

Affirmative	Negative	
	Full form	**Short form**
I played	I did not play	I didn't play
you played	you did not play	you didn't play
he played	he did not play	he didn't play
she played	she did not play	she didn't play
it played	it did not play	it didn't play
we played	we did not play	we didn't play
you played	you did not play	you didn't play
they played	they did not play	they didn't play

1 We use the simple past for actions which happened at a definite time in the past: we know when they happened and often add a time expression: **Last Saturday I visited the Bakers.**

2 We form the simple past affirmative of regular verbs by adding **-ed, -d** or **-ied**, and the form is the same for all persons.

3 We form the negative with the simple past **did not / didn't** + the base form of the verb: **I didn't play football.** We *never* say ~~I didn't played.~~

4 Look at the spelling of some regular verbs in the simple past:

Verb + *-ed*	Verb ending in 'e' + *-d*	Verb ending in 'y' – *ied*	Verb with one syllable, 1 vowel + 1 consonant
clean — clean**ed**	like — like**d**	carry — carr**ied**	drop — drop**ped**
open — open**ed**	move —move**d**	cry — cr**ied**	plan — plan**ned**
rain — rain**ed**	type — type**d**	tidy — tid**ied**	shop — shop**ped**
stay — stay**ed**	use — use**d**	try — tr**ied**	stop — stop**ped**

1 *Correct these sentences.*

1 Captain Strong visited his family last Saturday.

   Wrong. He didn't visit his family. He visited the Bakers.

2 He visited them a month ago.

   ....

3 They didn't have a very good time.

   ....

4 Captain Strong played tennis with Dad and John.

   ....

5 He played football with Mum and Liz.

   ....

6 John tidied his room.

   ....

2 *Say the simple past forms of these verbs with your teacher.*
Then write them in the correct boxes.

clean ✔	wash ✔	visit ✔	cry	stop	tidy	listen	ask
look	paint	open	talk	want	move	watch	hate
wait	play	cook	need	climb	type	use	taste
show	help	try	miss	rain	snow	like	drop

1 │ We say these with a '*d*' sound at the end:

   cleaned, ...

   ....

2 │ We say these with a '*t*' sound at the end:

   washed, ...

   ....

3 │ We say these with an '*id*' sound at the end:

   visited, ...

   ....

Interrogative	Short answers	
	Affirmative	**Negative**
did I help?	Yes, I did.	No, I didn't.
dld you help?	Yes, you did.	No, you didn't.
did he help?	Yes, he did.	No, he didn't.
did she help?	Yes, she did.	No, she didn't.
did it help?	Yes, it did.	No, it didn't.
did we help?	Yes, we did.	No, we didn't.
did you help?	Yes, you did.	No, you didn't.
did they help?	Yes, they did.	No, they didn't.

1 We form questions with **did +** base form of the verb: **Did you tidy your room?** We do *not* say ~~Did you tidied ... ?~~

2 In short **Yes / No** answers, we use **did / didn't** and leave out the rest of the sentence: **Did you help? Yes, I did. / No, I didn't.**

3 **ago** = 'back from now'. We use it with phrases to refer to the past: **a week ago, a month ago, 5 years ago.**

3 *Ask and answer questions. Then write them.*

1 I cleaned my teeth yesterday (he? ✔)
   Did he clean his teeth? — Yes, he did.
   ....

2 She played tennis last week. (they? ✗)
   Did they play tennis? — No, they didn't.
   ....

3 He visited America last year. (you? ✗)
   ....

4 They stayed in London last month. (she? ✔)
   ....

5 I helped my father last weekend. (you? ✔)
   ....

6 We watched TV yesterday. (he? ✗)
   ....

4 *Finish these sentences using the word* ago. *Say and write them.*

1 Today is Friday. Tuesday was <u>three days ago</u>.

2 Today is Saturday. Last Saturday was ....

3 This month is April. March was ....

4 This year is 19... . The year 1992 was ....

5 Today is April 10th. April 3rd was ....

6 Today is Friday. Last Sunday was ....

5 *What did they do? When did they do it? Look at the pictures. Ask and answer questions. Then write them.*

1 last weekend / visit

What did Captain Strong do last weekend?

He visited the Bakers.

2 three days ago / cook

....

....

....

3 yesterday / play

....

....

....

4 a week ago / tidy

....

....

....

5 last weekend / clean

....

....

....

6 four days ago / wash

....

....

....

25 Simple past with irregular verbs

Mammoths didn't fly

LIZ: What do you know about mammoths?

JOHN: They were big animals like elephants. They lived a long time ago.

LIZ: Yes. Look!

JANE: Some mammoths flew in the air.

LIZ: Don't be silly! They didn't fly. You're talking about dinosaurs.
Some dinosaurs flew, some swam, some ran.
But mammoths? They didn't fly and they didn't swim.

JOHN: And they didn't eat meat. They ate grass and they had
two large tusks three metres long.

Affirmative	Negative	
	Full form	**Short form**
I ran	I did not run	I didn't run
you ran	you did not run	you didn't run
he ran	he did not run	he didn't run
she ran	she did not run	she didn't run
it ran	it did not run	it didn't run
we ran	we did not run	we didn't run
you ran	you did not run	you didn't run
they ran	they did not run	they didn't run

1 We do not form the simple past of irregular verbs by adding **-ed,** and there are no rules. Each has its own form, and you have to learn them all by heart, but like regular verbs the form *is* the same for all persons.

2 We form the negative and question with the simple past **did not / didn't** + the base form of the verb, just as with regular verbs: **Did they fly? They didn't fly.** We *never* say ~~Did they flew? They didn't flew.~~

1 *Here are some irregular verbs. Match the infinitives (on the left) and their past forms (on the right). Write them below.*

bring ✔	eat ✔	run	drank	went	stood
buy	fly	see	lost	swam	wrote
catch	get up	spend	caught	bought	brought ✔
do	give	stand	ate ✔	flew	gave
drink	go	swim	got up	spent	ran
drive	lose	write	saw	did	drove

bring – brought, eat – ate,

....

....

....

....

....

2 *Fill in the blanks with affirmative and negative simple past forms.*

1 He ....*drank*..... some milk: he .....*didn't drink*..... any water. (drink)

2 She only .... $1: she .... $10. (spend)

3 I .... some elephants: I .... any lions. (see)

4 They .... in the sea: they .... in the lake. (swim)

5 We .... to France: we .... to Italy. (fly)

3 *Fill in the blanks with the correct simple past form of the verbs in brackets.*

1 Mammoths ..*were*.. big animals like elephants. (be)

2 Mammoths .... 100 years ago. (not live)

3 Mammoths .... a long time ago. (live)

4 Some dinosaurs .... in the air and some .... in the sea. (fly / swim)

5 Mammoths .... in the sea and they .... in the air. (not swim / not fly)

6 Mammoths .... meat. They .... grass. (not eat / eat)

7 They .... two large tusks about three metres long. (have)

Interrogative	Short answers	
	Affirmative	**Negative**
did I run?	Yes, I did.	No, I didn't.
did you run?	Yes, you did.	No, you didn't.
did he run?	Yes, he did.	No, he didn't.
did she run?	Yes, she did.	No, she didn't.
did it run?	Yes, it did.	No, it didn't.
did we run?	Yes, we did.	No, we didn't.
did you run?	Yes, you did.	No, you didn't.
did they run?	Yes, they did.	No, they didn't.

In short **Yes / No** answers, we use the verb **did / didn't** and leave out the rest of the sentence: **Did he catch a mouse? Yes, he did. / No, he didn't.**

4 *Mike is asking Liz about yesterday. Read these sentences and complete the conversation.*

- Mum and Dad bought some new shoes, John bought a computer game, and Mum gave Jane a book about dinosaurs.

- Me? I didn't have any money. I spent all my money last week.

- I went to town with Mum and Dad, John and Jane. ✔

- No, I didn't. It was a horrible day! — And it rained!

MIKE: Where did you go yesterday, Liz?

LIZ: *I went to town with Mum and Dad, John and Jane.* ....

MIKE: What did you all do?

LIZ: ....

MIKE: And what did *you* buy?

LIZ: ....

MIKE: So did you enjoy it?

LIZ: ....

5 *Ask and answer questions. Then write them.*

1

The cat / catch / a spider yesterday?

– No / it / catch / a mouse

<u>Did the cat catch a spider</u>

<u>yesterday?</u>

<u>– No, it didn't. It caught</u>

<u>a mouse.</u>

2

you / go / to London last year?

– No / I / go / to Athens

....

....

....

....

3

she / write / to John last week?

– No / she / write / to Jason

....

....

....

....

4

he / buy / a camera last month?

– No / he / buy / a computer

....

....

....

....

5

they / get up / at 8 o'clock yesterday?

– No / they / get up / at 7 o'clock

....

....

....

....

6

you / lose / your camera last weekend?

– No / I / lose / my English book

....

....

....

....

26 Simple past – regular and irregular

Jane wrote to Jason

Jason is staying with his aunt in Scotland. Jane wrote this letter to him.

Dear Jason,
    Are you enjoying your summer holiday? We are.
    Last Friday Dad took us to London for the day. He drove us there in his new car. Mum stayed at home for a rest! So Dad had a lot to do!
    We went to a special insect exhibition. It was great! We arrived at 11 in the morning and left at about 3 in the afternoon. We all enjoyed it – even Liz, and she usually gets bored quickly! The exhibition was all about insects – really big models of cockroaches, flies, bees...
    We studied everything and touched everything. We had a great time!
    See you soon.
    Jane

1 *Look at the past forms of these regular and irregular verbs.*

Regular verbs	Irregular verbs
enjoyed liked lived	drive – drove leave – left
stayed studied touched	go – went take – took
cried, cleaned	catch – caught

Now put the past forms of these verbs into the correct list.

cry ✔   clean ✔   catch ✔   move   open   play   drink   show   buy   stop
do   type   tidy   eat   try   visit   bring   wash   fly   watch

2 *Correct these sentences.*

1 Last Friday Mum took the children to London.

   Wrong. Dad took the children to London.

2 They went to London on the train.

   ....

3 Mum went to a friend's house for the day.

   ....

4 They went to the shops.

   ....

   ....

5 They arrived at the exhibition at 9.

   ....

   ....

6 They left at about 2 in the afternoon.

   ....

   ....

The children stayed here last Friday.

No, they didn't stay here. Dad took them to London.

Verb	Affirmative	Negative	Interrogative	Short answers
stay	stayed	didn't stay	did you stay?	Yes, I did. / No, I didn't.
take	took	didn't take	did you take?	Yes, I did. / No, I didn't.
have	had	didn't have	did you have?	Yes, I did. / No, I didn't.
be	was / were	wasn't / weren't	were you?	Yes, I was. / No, I wasn't.

3 *Ask and answer questions. Then write them.*

1 Where / Dad / take / children?

   Where did Dad take the children? – He took them to London.

2 Mum / stay / home?   Did Mum stay at home? – Yes, she did.

3 How / Dad / drive / them there?   ....

4 Which exhibition / they / go to?   ....

5 they / arrive / 10 in the morning?   ....

6 When / they / leave / the exhibition?   ....

4 *How did the children, Captain Strong and the animals help?*
Look at the picture. Then say and write sentences.

The children helped Dad in the garden. Liz picked the apples.

....

....

....

....

....

5 *Fill in the blanks with the correct simple past forms of the verbs in brackets.*

The first man on the Moon

Neil Armstrong 1.<u>was</u>. (be) the first man on the

Moon. He 2.......... (be) an American astronaut and in

1969 he 3.......... (fly) to the Moon in the Apollo 11

spaceship with Buzz Aldrin and Mike Collins. They

4.......... (leave) Earth on 16 July 1969 and 5..........

(land) on the Moon on 21 July. This is what they

6.......... (see) from their spaceship. Neil Armstrong

7.......... (stand) on the Moon on 21 July 1969.

6 **About you**

Answer these questions with full sentences.

1 When (or how long ago) did you
   last visit an exhibition or a museum?
   ....
   ....

2 Who did you go with?
   ....

3 Did you have a good time?
   ....

4 What did you do? (Write 2 or
   3 things.)
   ....
   ....

Prepositions of place – in, on, at, to

They had a fantastic time in Greece

LIZ: Where's Mary?

JOHN: She's in Greece.
She always goes there
for her holidays with her mum
and dad.

LIZ: Where do they stay?

JOHN: They don't always stay in the same place.
Two years ago they stayed in a little village
near Kalamata.

LIZ: Where's that?

JOHN: It's in the south of Greece.

LIZ: They're lucky!

JOHN: And last year they stayed in a villa
at the seaside.

LIZ: Where?

JOHN: On an island called Corfu.

LIZ: Did they enjoy it?

JOHN: Of course they enjoyed it.
They had a fantastic time.

Prepositions of place – in, on

in the box, **in** the room, **in** the hotel
in the street, **in** Bond Street
in Athens, **in** London, **in** England, **in** Europe
in the north / south / east / west of the country
on the table, **on** the floor
on an island, **on** the island of Corfu, **on** the coast

---

1 *Ask and answer these questions about Mary and her family.
Then write the answers.*

1 Where is Mary at the moment? *She's in Greece.* ....

2 Do Mary and her parents always stay in the same place ? ....

....

3 Where did they stay two years ago?   ....

4 Where is Kalamata?   ....

5 What did they stay in last year – a hotel or villa? Where?   ....

....

2 Mary is writing to Liz from Greece. Fill in the blanks with at, in or on.

Prepositions of place – *at*
at the door, **at** the window **at** the seaside, **at** the beach, **at** 29 Oxford Street

Prepositions of place — *to and at*	
1	**to** the shops He's cycling **to** the post office now. **to** the bank
2	**to** school He walked **to** work yesterday. **to** church She was **at** school / **at** work last week.
3	They were **at** home yesterday. She went / came / walked / ran home.

Dear Liz,

We arrived here three days ago. It's fantastic! We're staying (1)....in.... a beautiful villa (2)........... Corinth. It's a small place (3).......... the coast near Athens.

On the way here we stayed (4)......... a very nice hotel (5)........... Athens for two nights.

The weather is great – it's hot and sunny every day. We were (6)........... the beach all day yesterday. It was lovely!

See you soon.

Love,

Mary

3 Fill in the blanks with in, at, on, to, or '—'.

1 We stayed ...at.... home yesterday.

2 My uncle and aunt live .... Australia.

3 John wasn't .... school yesterday.

4 Brighton is a town .... the south of England.

5 Brighton is .... the south coast.

6 They always stay .... the same hotel for their holiday.

7 They're going .... work early today.

8 My grandparents live .... London.

9 Dad walked .... home from work yesterday.

28 *going to*

I'm going to be rich!

JANE: I'm going to be a nurse.

JOHN: Why?

JANE: Because nurses help people.

LIZ: Well, I'm not going to be a nurse.

JOHN: Why not?

LIZ: I'm not going to help people.
I'm going to help animals.
I'm going to be a vet.

JANE: What about you, John?
What are you going to be?

JOHN: Me? I'm going to be rich!
I'm going to buy a big house
and a fast car!

Affirmative Full form / Short form	Negative Full form / Short form	Future time expressions
I am / I'm going to play	I am not / I'm not going to play	tomorrow
you are / you're going to play	you are not / you aren't going to play	this evening
he is / he's going to play	he is not / he isn't going to play	on Saturday
she is / she's going to play	she is not / she isn't going to play	next Sunday
it is / it's going to play	it is not / it isn't going to play	next weekend
we are / we're going to play	we are not / we aren't going to play	next week
you are / you're going to play	you are not / you aren't going to play	next month
they are / they're going to play	they are not / they aren't going to play	next year

We use **be going to** + base form of the verb to express 1) a future intention (**I'm going to be a nurse.**) or a plan (**We're going to see our Gran tomorrow.**), or 2) something that is certain to happen, as in **It's going to snow. Look at the sky.**

1 *Fill in the blanks with* is going to, are going to, isn't going to *or* aren't going to.

1 Jane *is going to* be a nurse.

2 Liz .... be a nurse. She .... be a vet.

3 John .... be rich. He .... help people.

   He .... buy a big house and a fast car.

4 Together Jane and Liz .... help people and animals.

5 John .... be a poor man!

Interrogative	Short answers	
	Affirmative	**Negative**
am I going to help?	Yes, I am.	No, I'm not.
are you going to help?	Yes, you are.	No, you aren't.
is he going to help?	Yes, he is.	No, he isn't.
is she going to help?	Yes, she is.	No, she isn't.
is it going to help?	Yes, it is.	No, it isn't.
are we going to help?	Yes, we are.	No, we aren't.
are you going to help?	Yes, you are.	No, you aren't.
are they going to help?	Yes, they are.	No, they aren't.

Are you going to be a vet?

No, I'm not.

2 *Look at the Bakers' family diary for next week. What are they all going to do? Ask and answer questions. Then write them.*

1 (Liz / help Dad / Sunday)   Is Liz going to help Dad on Sunday? — No, she isn't. She's going to write some letters.

2 (John and Jane / help Dad / Monday)   Are John and Jane going to help Dad on Monday? — Yes, they are.

SUNDAY	Liz — write some letters
MONDAY	John and Jane — help Dad
TUESDAY	Dad — fly to Italy
WEDNESDAY	John — stay with friends
THURSDAY	Mum — go shopping

3 (Dad / fly to Greece / Tuesday)

....

4 (John / stay with friends / Wednesday)   ....

....

5 (Mum / see Liz's teacher / Thursday)   ....

....

3 *Fill in the blanks with* Why? Why not? because *and a correct form of* going to — am going to, aren't going to, *etc.*

1 MARY: I am going to be an air hostess.

JASON: Why?

MARY: Because they fly all over the world.

2 MOG: He .... a vet.

SCAMP: Why not?

MOG: Because he doesn't like animals!

3 DAD: We .... have a picnic.

MUM: ....

DAD: .... it's a sunny day.

4 JOHN: Liz .... get up early.

MIKE: ....

JOHN: .... she's very tired.

going to, present simple and present continuous

I'm going to be a stunt woman!

INTERVIEWER: Pam, you're one of the top stunt women in Britain. What does a stunt woman do?

PAM: Well, a stunt woman usually works for a film company or a television company. A lot of actresses don't do dangerous things. So I do things for them.

INTERVIEWER: For example?

PAM: I drive fast cars. I jump out of planes with a parachute, I ride horses – things like that. And last week I fell out of a window; but it wasn't dangerous. The glass was special material called sugar glass. It broke easily.

INTERVIEWER: And what are you doing now?

PAM: I'm just waiting and having a snack. In five minutes' time I'm going to jump off that building.

INTERVIEWER: Wow!

I'm not going to be a vet. I'm going to be a stunt woman instead!

Present simple

What **does** a stunt woman **do**?
She **drives** fast cars.

Present continuous

What **are** you **doing** now?
I'm waiting and (**I'm**) **having** a snack.

going to future

What **are** you **going to be** (in the future)?
I'm **going to be** a stunt woman.

1 *Ask and answer these questions about Pam. Then write the answers.*

1 What does Pam do?

   She's a stunt woman. ....

2 What does Pam do as a stunt woman?

   ....

3 What did she do last week?

   ....

4 Why wasn't it dangerous?

   ....

5 What is she doing at this moment?

   ....

6 What is she going to do in five minutes' time?

   ....

7 Liz is not going to be a vet now. What is she going to do instead?

   ....

2 *What do they usually do? What are they going to do?*
Say and write sentences.

	USUALLY	NEXT WEEK
John	play tennis	play basketball
Liz	cook lunch	cook the evening meal
Mum	clean bathroom	clean the kitchen
Mog	eat fish	eat meat

1 John usually plays tennis , but next week he's going to play basketball .

2 Liz .... , but next ....

3 Mum .... , but ....

4 Mog .... , ...

Did you see that programme on TV last night all about real operations? It was great. I'm going to be a surgeon.

But you don't like blood. We watched *Dracula* and you were ill!

Oh, that was different. That wasn't real. A surgeon operates on real people.

Sometimes I don't understand girls.

3 *Ask and answer questions. Then write them.*

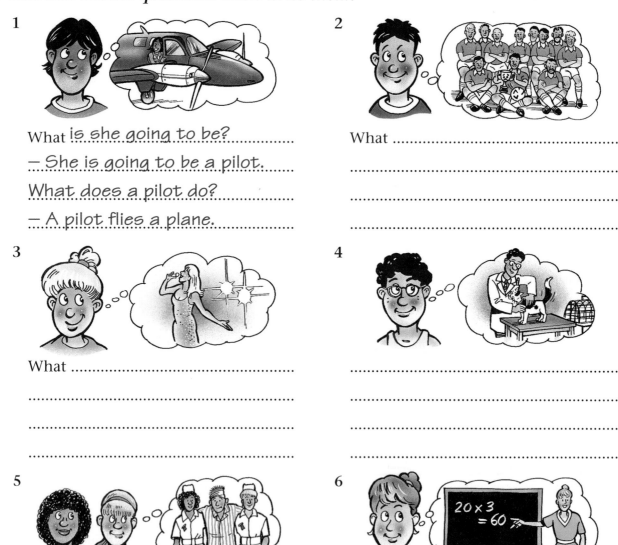

1
What is she going to be?
— She is going to be a pilot.
What does a pilot do?
— A pilot flies a plane.

2
What ....
....
....
....

3
What ....
....
....
....

4
....
....
....
....

5
....
....
....
....

6
....
....
....
....

4 About you

You're writing your first letter to Pat, an English, American, Canadian or Australian pen friend. Answer these questions with full answers.

Write your own address here

Write the date here

Paragraph 1

What's your name?

How old are you?

Where do you live?

Who do you live with?

What school do you go to?

What lessons do you like?

What sports do you play?

Paragraph 2

What do you usually do at the weekend?

What did you do last weekend?

What are you going to do next weekend?

Paragraph 3

What do you usually do in the holidays?

Dear Pat,

Please write soon.
Best wishes,

Irregular verbs

Base form	Simple past
be	was / were
become	became
bring	brought
buy	bought
catch	caught
do	did
drink	drank
drive	drove
eat	ate
fly	flew
get up	got up
give	gave
go	went
have	had
leave	left
lose	lost
run	ran
say	said
see	saw
spend	spent
stand	stood
swim	swam
take	took
write	wrote